PLAZA

Praise for
The Retirement Activities Guide

"Bruce Juell has taken a big step in helping the future of an aging society by applying supply-side economics to the topic of retirement. He has "supplied" many ideas as inspiration for healthy retirees to be more active and productive for themselves and for society."

> – Arthur Laffer, Founder, Laffer Associates
> Creator of the Laffer Curve

"I hope that many of us who are retiring from our principal lifetime roles will read and consider the many thought provoking ideas in *The Retirement Activities Guide* as they explore ways they can retire in a healthy, active, and purposeful way."

> – John McArthur, Dean Emeritus
> The Harvard Business School

"To too many retirees, the only 'M' word is 'Money.' Bruce helps us find "Meaning" in our new way of living—a way to enrich and enjoy our available hours."

> – Anthony Frank, retired
> CEO, First Nationwide Bank
> Postmaster General of the United States

"Professionals in most sports, like professionals in any other field, know that their playing or coaching careers can only last so long. Bruce has provided us with a broad array of ideas for them to consider; ways they can use their talents and influence to help themselves and others."

> – Jim Mora, former head coach
> New Orleans Saints, Indianapolis Colts

"The Retirement Activities Guide is one that every person who is either retired or soon will be needs to read. In a nutshell, its message is that many retirees are desiring to do more than they are currently doing (or planning to do when they retire) in order to continue to make a difference in the world in terms of activities that will be challenging, creative, fulfilling and legacy-making. Even a small increase in productivity of this huge population can have a profound impact on society. This book provides practical steps on how to get involved. It is a must read."

      – Harold Koenig, M.D.
      Professor of Psychiatry & Behavioral Sciences, Duke University
      Author, *Purpose and Power in Retirement*

"Bruce Juell has shown creativity in bringing together a broad range of ideas and information that is helpful for people to consider as they plan their retirement. He gives us some guidance on living to be creative, and helps us find challenging "second careers" while at the same time leaving a legacy in the form of a contribution to a strong and healthy society. The book is a valuable assist in finding meaningful retirement activity."

      – Alan J. Rowe, Emeriti Professor
      University of Southern California
      Author, *Creative Intelligence*

"There are many things to consider when individuals start to plan their transition into retirement. *The Retirement Activities Guide* can help them by giving concrete examples of things they can consider for challenging and fulfilling use of the many years ahead of them."

      – Nancy K. Schlossberg, Author,
      Retire Smart, Retire Happy
      Finding Your True Path
      Professor Emerita, University of Maryland

The Retirement Activities Guide

165 Ideas for Finding Fulfillment and Meaning

Things To Do When Golf and Grandkids Aren't Enough

Bruce Juell

3rd Age Press
Rolling Hills Estates, California

Publisher's Cataloging in Publication Data

Juell, Bruce

  The retirement activities guide: 165 ideas for finding fulfillment and meaning: things to do when golf and grandkids aren't enough / by Bruce Juell. — 1st ed, — Rolling HIlls Estates, Calif. : 3rd Age Press, 2006.

    p.; cm.

  "A retired corporate executive provides a guidebook to a wide range of ideas and activities for retirees and those thinking about their next 'career'."
  Includes bibliographical references and index.
  ISBN: 0-9765791-3-8
  ISBN-13: 978-0-9765791-3-7

  1. Retirement—Planning. 2. Retirement. 3. Retirees. 4. Older people—Psychology.
  5. Retirees—Employment. 6. Older people—Employment. 7. Quality of life.
  I. Title.

HQ1062.J84 2006   2005901730
306.3/8—dc22   0512

FIRST EDITION

Design and layout by Robert Goodman, Silvercat™, San Diego, California
Printed in the United States of America

This book is dedicated with love to

Jean Haynes Juell

my loyal and hard working partner
for the past fifty years, the mother
of our five children and the co-grandparent
of our eight 'great' grandkids.

Contents

Acknowledgments

*T*his book is built upon the results of work that many have done before me. My appreciation applies not only to the research and studies performed by the many authors of books on aging and retirement, but the effort expended and success that they have had in getting their work into print and distributed.

Their efforts have allowed me to skim over many of the positive and negative aspects of retirement in this book and focus on developing information on a wide range of activities in which healthy, financially able retirees may find fulfillment and meaning to enrich their lives, and the lives of others.

Getting Started

A journey of a thousand miles begins with a single step.
∿ Lao-Tzu

Whenever someone has trouble getting started on a small project or a major life decision, the best counsel is typically "do something—anything" to get into gear. Picking up this book and thinking about these ideas can get a reader's imagination started. Even if the result is doing something entirely different than anything presented here, it will have fulfilled its mission.

Introduction

*T*his book is intended for those who are approaching, or have entered that period in their lives when they don't have to go to work on a regular basis, and are looking for interesting and fulfilling things to do with those extra hours.

Retirement can be a traumatic experience. People who have been active in a career, with their own businesses or as participants in other organizations, suddenly discover that they don't know what to do with themselves. They can't go to the office, they can't visit customers, they can't send e-mails to vendors.

For many, the initial plan is to play golf, travel and enjoy the grandkids and the garden. But after a while, these activities don't provide the meaning or fulfillment that they are looking for.

This book recognizes that we are all going to live a lot longer, and be much healthier and probably more affluent in retirement than were our parents. A person who retires at age sixty-five can expect to live another twenty years, on average, and has a fifty percent probability of living past eighty-five. Met Life projects that a sixty-five year-old couple has a twenty-five percent chance of living to age ninety-seven.

These data mean that about twenty-five percent of the average retiree's life will be spent in retirement; that their "second career" will be about fifty percent as long as their primary career.

A recent AARP article states that we will be living not only longer but more fully as we age. They talk about an increase in 'active' life expectancy. Quality of life is the big issue. Are we going to have large numbers of very old people who are vigorous, reasonably healthy, involved and productive? Or are we going to have a large percentage of people who are lonely, bored, not very healthy and depressed?

A new book, *Younger Next Year: A Guide to Living Like 50 Until You're 80 and Beyond,* by Chris Crowley and Henry S. Lodge makes the point that two of the keys to keeping your body from decaying are having a "real engagement with living" and a related attitude, "emotional commitment."

We strongly believe that individuals who are involved in meaningful, fulfilling activities will beat the odds. Having purpose provides the motivation to get up in the morning, to take care of one's self and the opportunity to be in active, supportive relationships. In short, to live richer lives.

This book is built on a base established by the many books on retirement and aging that provide information on finance, health, the law, places to live and the various psychological aspects of leaving a career and transitioning into a new life. It is a "what to-" as contrasted to a "how to-" book. It is a start on an answer to the question, "What's next?"

The purpose of the book is to provide exposure to a variety of ideas; to get the reader thinking about things they might want to consider. It can serve as a catalyst. Readers might find just the thing; more likely, they will see something that triggers their imagination and creative spark, which will then lead them to a beginning of an answer.

How This Book Came To Be

This book is the result of my own quest for a 'post-retirement' mission. It is based on my experiences and contacts during a varied business career and extensive exploration into the attitudes, expectations and desires of retiring and retired colleagues and associates, as well as those of friends and neighbors.

As I arrived at that magical time when I no longer needed to perform for others, I began looking for something new and rewarding in my life. I had had a fulfilling career, and now I had the prospect of a long period of freedom in which I could do almost anything I wanted.

I realized that I could be looking forward to another thirty years ahead of me. What could I do that would be interesting, challenging, fulfilling, important and enriching?

Once I identified this challenge, it dawned on me that I was not alone. There had to be millions of individuals out there dealing with the same general set of questions.

I have been a practicing demographer for the better part of my career. As the Chief Executive Officer of Six Flags, Inc., the second largest amusement park company in the United States, I found myself focused on the problem of attracting and entertaining thousands of pre-teens, teens and young adults to our parks. The baby boom group was key to our market.

As that group grew older, I was concerned with the problem of continuing to attract them as they aged. I became interested in the Del Webb Corporation because of their position in the casino business. What could be a better 'amusement park' for adults than a casino, particularly if we could bring the family entertainment element to those casinos, as the new Circus Circus was doing.

I was not able to convince our shareholders that they wanted to be in the 'sin city' business, but in the process I was asked to join the Board of Directors of Del Webb Corporation. I then became a minor expert in a new set of demographics, that of those retiring and how they could be attracted to become owners and residents of the Del Webb Sun City projects.

Now that the baby boomer group is beginning to turn fifty-five and merging into the retiree market, it has become clear to me that this represents both a problem and an opportunity of major scale. In 2030, when all of the seventy-seven million baby boomers have retired, there are projected to be twice as many retirees as there are today, but only eighteen percent more workers to support their Social Security benefits. This demographic overload is the problem side.

My perspective is quite different. I see the glass as half full, not half empty. I believe that this group has the potential of being a major contributor to society. I observed that while the consensus view about retirees is that they are a burden to society, particularly as they extend their life span, they could also be an important resource. I concluded that I might be particularly qualified to help develop some meaningful approaches and solutions on the positive side.

Many of these individuals are well educated, have held responsible management, professional or craftsman positions, and because of the way they are taking care of themselves, they are going to be around and active for many more years.

With this in mind, I decided that my vision for the rest of my life would be to help bring the potential of this new productivity to a higher level of visibility and actuality.

While seniors and retirees do represent a large market with a great deal of spending power, I was not particularly attracted to the idea of selling this group something. I had been doing that all my life; I wanted to do something more significant, more meaningful to me.

My first step was to develop an Internet website, which I launched as CreativeSeniors.com. It was a way to present my basic idea and goals, and to attempt to begin recruiting others to the cause. However, while my general concept is valid and significant, it is somewhat vague. I needed to come up with a more specific first step.

I spoke to my peers—members of the Young Presidents Organization and its alumni group, the Chief Executives Organization; my McKinsey & Company fellow alumni; the University of Southern California alumni organization; the California Club; my golf club—and to my friends and neighbors. Most of them agreed that it was certainly a big group that I was addressing, but when I asked them about their plans, I typically received a blank look.

Most of these individuals had had full and varied careers, many served on for-profit and nonprofit boards of directors and most of them played golf and traveled a lot. While some of them acknowledged being somewhat bored, or even depressed, "I am busier than I have ever been," was a more common response.

However, with my consulting and market research background, I delved further. I spoke to their wives. "I wish he would find something to do to get him out of the house," was a typical comment. "For better or worse, but never for lunch" was their battle cry.

I concluded that the first thing that was needed was a broad range of ideas for these individuals to consider, from which they could develop their own vision of what they might do when they realize they needed greater fulfillment. This gave birth to this guidebook.

The idea was that while an individual may have difficulty describing, even to themselves, what they might want to do, with the help of a large number of alternatives, they may 'know it when they see it.'

This book is intended for anyone who is looking for something more fulfilling in their lives. I hope it is as effective and useful as I believe it can be.

What Do We Call It?

One of the major problems for anyone discussing or writing about this important stage in life is nomenclature. If we call it 'retirement,' many will contend that they are not 'retired,' even at age eighty. If we try to base it on the arrival at a certain age we find that many are 'retired' at age fifty, others are fully employed at age seventy-five.

Sixty-five has been the standard for the age of retirement for many years. However, AARP uses fifty as their criteria for initial membership. As the largest organization of its type, it has by default defined the leading edge of retirement. Another important age cut is that of Social Security payment eligibility, which begins at sixty-two.

The French have developed the idea of the *le troisieme age,* the third age. Other names that have evolved include:

Second act	Eldering
Second half	Old people
Second maturity	Older people
Second wind	Older Americans
Senescence	Old farts
Middlescence	Geezers
Senior citizens	Geezer Glut
Mature Market	Primetime
Elderhood	Previously fully employed

50 plus	Post-Work
Gray Panthers	Post-Career
Renaissance	Halftime
OPAL's (Old People with Active Lives)	
Elder Americans	

We have played with the idea of a new word, something related to 'redeployment' or 'repositioning' or 're-tired' (as in putting on new treads). So far, we have found nothing worth trademarking.

The problem is similar to that of writers wanting a single pronoun to refer to males and females—he or she, her or him—as yet no one has come up with a combination or compromise that works. The feminist movement came up with Ms. as a way of avoiding the Miss or Mrs. embarrassment if one was wrong.

The closest we been able to come to narrowing down the naming issue is the phrase "retired or retiring." So that is what we will tend to use here.

Finding Meaning, Fulfillment

The striving to find a meaning in one's life is the primary motivational force in man.. It is the search for meaning that gives life its substance.

~ Victor Frankl

*T*his guidebook has been developed to provide ideas and to motivate individuals to take an active role in directing and managing their own retirement; to show them ways to plan and implement a program of fulfilling, rewarding and sociably useful activity for their post-retirement years.

Fulfillment is a relative, or contextual term. Like 'happiness,' it depends on who is experiencing it, or trying to experience it. It's a goal. And, the goal of the book is to get the reader to work at finding fulfillment, making the attempt, striving for it. It's the journey that is important. Once you are fulfilled, what else is there?

These ideas should not be viewed as 'shoulds,' but rather sources of inspiration; ways to start thinking both inside and outside the box about what might appeal to individuals who do not already have their "Third Act" written.

Too many times individuals retire and begin coasting. They welcome the freedom of choice, the opportunity to play golf whenever they want to, to travel, spend time with their grandkids or to just relax. By the time they get around to deciding that these activities are not sufficiently enriching, that they would like to do something they might leave as a memorial, it may be too late.

We never know how long we really have. That is one of the exciting aspects of this whole process. However, the sooner we get started, the more satisfying the results can be.

And the longer we will have to enjoy them.

Stewardship

Much will be required of the person entrusted with much,
and still more will be demanded of the person entrusted with
more.

~ Luke 12:48

*D*espite my admonition that I do not want to lay any *shoulds* on the readers of this guide, I must let you know my personal perspective. I believe in the whole process of using one's life as productively as possible; to be good stewards of what we have been given.

We enter this world with nothing, we have been loaned our lives and all of the gifts we have received. The Bible advises us that faithful use of one's gifts will lead to participation in the fullness of the kingdom, lazy inactivity to exclusion from it.

Regardless of one's religious beliefs, or lack thereof, these concepts are worthy of reflection. We must be grateful for the gifts we have received, responsible and wise in what we do with them, generous in sharing them with others. We must leave the world a better place.

Legacy

Whenever a U.S. president is discussed, it is common for us to consider his legacy—what did he do that left his mark on the Country, on the world, on society; what will he be remembered for?

We all want to be remembered. As we age, and attend more and more funeral and memorial services, we have the opportunity each time to reflect on our own lives and how we would like to be remembered.

It may be, once a person has retired, that he or she has accomplished that memorable activity, or achieved that goal for which they would like to be remembered. However, retirement gives us the opportunity to consider the topic in more depth, to think about other things we might do to add to that speech that your friends and family will have a chance to make when it is your turn.

Think about the legacy that you would like to leave—and then start working on it.

First Things First

*B*efore getting terribly excited about doing something new and different, anyone with an interest in, or plans for, leaving full-time employment and taking on a new challenge needs to deal with some basics. These ideas assume that those basics have been taken care of.

We refer to the "Five F's" of retirement—Finance, Fitness, Family, Friends, and Fulfillment. The first four of these are critically important issues, topics that are covered well by many other books, Internet websites, magazine articles and commercial providers of services. We have not attempted to deal with them at any depth here.

This book is focused on the fifth element, Fulfillment. However, we would be remiss if we encourage the pursuit of our ideas if the other four areas had not been tended to.

First, make sure that your Financial house is in as good a shape as it can be, that you are tending to your health and Fitness, that your relationships with your Family and Friends are what they should be. Remember, make new friends, but keep the old . . .

With regard to Finance, some of the ideas presented here may involve an investment. Please think about ten times, and then take a cold shower, and talk to your significant others, before putting any of your hard earned assets that are not fully discretionary, at risk.

Finding Flow

*T*he typical attitude upon reaching retirement is that we no longer want to work; we want leisure. But leisure is basically what you do when no one is telling you what to do. Any activity can be a leisure activity as long as it is chosen freely and you enjoy doing it. For many people, what they used to consider work can be truly pleasurable, particularly if it takes them into the condition of 'flow.'

Flow is a concept that has been researched and developed in some detail in the book by that name, by Mihaly Csikszentimihaly. A person's most personally satisfying moments occur when they are doing something that they really enjoy; when their body and mind are being used to the fullest in solving a difficult task. It falls somewhere between boredom and anxiety, between being fully at rest and being fully stressed.

We are in flow when working on a project that requires our full attention and talents; when we are accomplishing something that is fulfilling because of its use of our skills and the satisfying results it will provide. In other words, it is work that we love to do.

Earlier in life we do many things because of responsibilities to others. When we retire, we typically do not have others telling us what to do, we have a great deal of freedom to do what we wish, so flow type activities must be internally or self generated. The individual then has a greater personal burden of finding activities or projects that can provide the joy of being in flow. That flow includes the satisfaction of exercising control over one's time and efforts, rather than being controlled by others.

The flow concept also suggests that passivity, or unchallenging activities, leads to disillusion, rather than gratification. Flow is the satisfaction that comes with the journey, not from arriving at the destination.

It's Never Too Late To Start

*T*he sooner you get started planning for your 'next act' the more productive and enriching it is apt to be. This process would ideally be given consideration while an individual is still actively employed and has the attitude that they are going to live forever.

By starting early, individuals can use the support system and contacts involved in their active careers to help pave the way for the anticipated new adventure. You may think you don't need to plan ahead. It may take that period after initial retirement to get the golf, travel, sleeping late, not shaving, time with the kids and grandkids out of the system, to decide that these activities are not enough. To realize that they may fill part of the day, but ultimately do not provide enough satisfaction, meaning or fulfillment.

So don't tell yourself, "I wish I had thought of this earlier." It's never too late—get on with it!

The Idea Behind These Ideas

*T*his guidebook is intended to give the reader some ideas and inspiration about things they might consider doing. The resources used in developing it include the personal experiences and observations of the author, the experiences of personal and professional acquaintances, and an extensive search of the literature and of Internet sites.

There is a wide spectrum of ideas presented here. Some of them are much more challenging than others. Many of the ideas are already developed programs that you can join with little or no imagination on your part. They don't require much more than a phone call or email contact to get into.

Most of the government supported programs are of that nature. It will require some tenacity to find the specific thing that appeals to you, but that is not much different than shopping for a new car or planning a trip with a travel agent.

Some of the ideas are smaller programs that others have initiated and may or may not represent something you can affiliate with. These are presented to give you some idea of what others have done; perhaps you may be motivated by, and can learn from, their experiences.

At the more creative end of the spectrum are ideas that are simply that, ideas. There are thousands of opportunities represented by problems that need addressing. The ways to capitalize on those opportunities or the road to getting those problems solved are not so clear. A problem or opportunity can represent a starting point for the individual with whom the issue resonates.

That individual must then figure out what he or she might want to do with regard to that idea, how they can get additional information and how they might proceed with a specific plan of action. The book tries to make some suggestions about this action planning process, but it will be up to the individual, or a group of like-minded individuals, to take specific action and see results.

The "Taking Action" section following the Ideas attempts to provide some thoughts and resources related to getting started on your new career.

A word of caution about the information presented here. The programs described may have changed since the book went to press, the funding for some may have dried up, government programs may have been cut. However, even if the program or idea has changed, it may still provide the inspiration for the reader to do something similar, or to help revive a worthy project.

Understanding Your Attitude

A human being can change his life by changing his attitude of mind.

~ William James

*F*or the user of this book of ideas, it is useful to understand where you are coming from; what your attitude is about this whole process of looking for new, exciting, meaningful things to do.

Dr. Nancy Schlossberg, in her book *Retire Smart Retire Happy* has identified and named different approaches or attitudes of people as they attempt to structure their lives in retirement. In their efforts to obtain the recognition, satisfaction, and meaning that they had received through their work, she indicates that most of the retirees fall into one of the following categories:

* *Continuers*—for whom identity in previous work, home or volunteer life is still in control;
* *Adventurers*—who have moved in new directions, whether paid or unpaid;
* *Searchers*—who are separating from the past but who have not yet found their place;
* *Easy Gliders*—who are content, enjoy retirement, go with whatever comes along; and

- *Retreaters*—who have given up on forging a new, rewarding life.

This book is ideally suited to the *Searcher* group; those who know they are looking for something meaningful and are eager to find it. However, we are also targeting the *Adventurers*, who have found things that interest them, but may be interested in alternatives or more challenging activities.

We also hope to tempt the *Easy Gliders* with some of our ideas; perhaps they can be persuaded to move into the *Searcher* mode as they find that their contentment is transient.

Finally, perhaps we can all help the *Retreaters* as we encounter them.

Ways To Use These Ideas

*. . . it is possible to change the world if one is determined
enough, and if one sees with sufficient clarity just what it is
that has to be changed.*

           ∽ Mma Ramotswe,
           The Kalahari Typing School For Men

In viewing the ideas presented here, readers have a number of ways to react to them. They can see them as specific suggestions, to accept or reject. We think of this as the direct approach.

They can read the material and decide that the specific program may not be appropriate for some reason, but with modification (change of venue, male rather than female, smaller rather than so big, etc.) it could be interesting and worth further investigation. We refer to this as the first derivative approach.

They can think, "I don't like the idea of being subsidized by my fellow taxpayers by going into a government sponsored program, but how about my starting something with similar goals, but without the taxpayer support, and the associated bureaucracy involved?" This we have called the free enterprise approach.

Or, they may read the suggestion, have it remind them of their old friend Joe Harris who used to do something like that, lost his shirt and went into something totally different. And decide that they would be interested in doing what finally made Joe happy. This is the second derivative, or Old Joe approach.

The point is that these are ideas, not floor plans. If something tickles your fancy, think about how you might build on the idea and do something with it. The more creativity you can apply, the more rewarding the outcome is apt to be.

Creativity

Imagination is more important than knowledge.
~ Albert Einstein

Creativity is an attitude, not an end result. We believe that keeping the creative juices flowing will go a long way toward improving your satisfaction with life, and with your having something exciting to get up for in the morning.

There is a chicken and egg aspect to creativity as it relates to getting involved in new activities later in life. If you are creative, it is easier and more rewarding to do new things; if you take on new and challenging activities it will sharpen your creative skills.

Dr. Gene Cohen, in his book *The Creative Age* states that 'the unique combination of age, experience and creativity can produce exciting inner growth and infinite potential' in the second half of life. He identifies four benefits of creativity: strengthening of our morale by altering the way we experience problems; a contribution to our physical health with a more positive outlook and sense of well being; enriched relationships; and leaving a legacy for our children and grandchildren in demonstrating what is possible as we age.

Alan Rowe, in his *Creative Intelligence*, states that those who dream and create will find new worlds to conquer. The capacity to learn and be creative extends far beyond the early years. Creative individuals question, explore outside their areas of expertise, and are willing to change their own views and the views of others.

Selection Criteria

 $\mathcal{E}$ ach reader will want to evaluate the individual ideas presented from his or her own perspective, personal background, interests and other motivating factors. Some of the criteria that might be used include the following:

- Fit with personal background
- Education
- Family interests
- Work experience
- Contacts
- Challenge provided
- Level of creativity involved
- Potential financial rewards, if important
- Help or value to society
- Potential for leaving a legacy
- Fitting with those things "you always wanted to do."

Applying these criteria, and others that readers will want to develop for themselves, is a very personal process. We do recommend that each reader think about those personal criteria before reviewing the ideas in detail. And continue to refine those criteria as they evaluate specific ideas.

Don't forget to include your family and 'significant others' in your thinking as you evaluate your personal criteria.

Important Tools

*T*he following are some basic resources you should be able to use effectively if you become serious about taking on a new, enriching project.

Your Local Library

A great place to start on any search is your local library. If you see a book on a topic that interests you, check that book out, but also look at other titles on the shelf near that book.

Also, look inside the 'copyright' page just before the table of contents and it will show the various subject headings related to that book. Use those subjects in the library computer index and you can find more books with content related to the one that initially appealed to you.

The periodical section of the library will provide magazines to browse through. And don't forget to talk to the reference librarian for further information. Most libraries also have provision for users to browse the library files at home by using the Internet.

The Internet

The whole job of looking for ideas, and for more information about those ideas has been revolutionized by the Internet. At first, the idea of using the Internet can be quite intimidating. If you haven't taken the big step, find a friend, neighbor, grandkid or a local adult education course to help you. Swallow hard and dive in!

You can get started using the Internet at your library for free, but you will soon decide to have your own system. Internet service is available for as little as $9.00 per month; faster broadband service (cable or DSL) can run about $40 per month.

Search Engines

Once you are into the Internet, the next challenge is to understand what your choices are among the search engines and how to use the ones you select. The number of items that a search will come up with will overwhelm you. As you become more sophisticated, your search will be more focused and your results will be more relevant. Again, don't be intimidated!

Your Computer

You will need a good, up-to-date computer to use the Internet, search engines and the email system that will be vital to your communication system. If your computer is more than four or five years old, we suggest that you not try to upgrade it; get a new one with the latest operating system and associated software. You will be able to get a system that will serve most of your needs for under $800.

Friends and Neighbors

Don't forget to use your acquaintances as important resources in your search process. The question, "So what are you doing now that you are retired?" is a good opportunity to respond with, "I am becoming an expert on the subject of _____. Do you know anyone who can help me?"

You will be surprised at how willing people are to help, and much of it will be valuable. Your friend might not have the answer, but the people they introduce you to might.

The best part of the process is the opportunity to strengthen old ties and develop many new friends.

Making Contact

Once you identify an activity that interests you, or that you want to learn more about, the place to start is probably the activity's website, if they have one. That site in turn might give you leads or ideas that take you to other related sites. If you want additional information of a general nature, you can email someone at the site (usually click on "Contact Us" on their website).

If you decide that you may want to get involved, we suggest a personal call to the person in charge. Email is easy to ignore, and it is usually handled by someone who may not give you the personal attention you should have. If the head person isn't available, his or her assistant can probably refer you to the right person, or see that your call is returned.

Don't get discouraged if you have some trouble making the right contact or getting the information you want. Many of the organizations are quite busy and you may need to be persistent if it is something you really care about. You can usually find some live person to give you insight, answer initial questions and ultimately get you to the right person.

Some of the sites' Internet addresses may have changed, or the site may no longer exist. We have not included the 'www.' in front of the website addresses, as these are typically not required. However, some sites will not come up unless you do have it included. So if the site you are interested in does not come up, add the 'www.' and it should work.

Be persistent. Just like with that pretty girl in high school, faint heart ne'er won fair lady!

The Ideas

*T*he basic activity ideas in this guide are organized into a number of fields and sub-fields of activity. Some of these are quite focused and clear, others are more ambiguous.

We recommend that the reader scan the entire list. This will help start the creative juices flowing. Even if you think you are interested in a specific type of activity, like mentoring, you will be reminded of other activities that might be equally inviting.

These are the basic groupings:

- Government Programs
- Volunteering Opportunities in the U.S.
- Volunteering Opportunities Abroad
- Mentoring, Helping Kids
- Religious, Faith Based, Spiritual
- Employment Opportunities
- Entrepreneuring, Business, New Ventures,
- Special Travel, Adventure
- Developing Relationships
- Learning, Education
- Writing, Arts, Literature
- Improving Your Community
- Healthcare, Medicine
- Find a Need and Fill It.

Many of the ideas could be positioned in more than one category, so be persistent. Each section has a number of ideas to consider and evaluate in light of your own interests.

As you think of other ideas that you think should be listed, please contact us with the information. See the Give Us Feedback section at the end of the book.

Enjoy the adventure!

Government Sponsored Programs

Federal Programs

The most highly organized and best funded programs for seniors or retirees are those available through the U.S. Government. Of course, these are also the most costly to the U.S. taxpayer.

The Older Americans Act was originally signed into law by Lyndon Johnson in 1965, with funding of $5 million. In 1988 it was funded at the level of $1 billion, and it was substantially amended in 2000, adding even more programs and cost. That amendment extended the life of the Act to 2005.

The various programs that have evolved under the Act are extensive. Many are not particularly appropriate for the healthy, active retiree. They are a means to assist and subsidize seniors that need help.

An overview of the programs, both Federal and state, that fall under the Older Americans Act is provided in an appendix to this book.

Two programs that fall under the USA Freedom program—RSVP and Volunteers for Prosperity—have been specifically identified in this book as appropriate for active creative seniors and are described in the following Ideas sections.

Other programs that are partially supported by the Act, and which are appropriate, are also included.

State Programs

Each of the United States has its own government sponsored volunteer programs. Many of these are directly related to and partially supported by the various Federal programs.

We have presented here some of the programs currently operating in California, as examples of the types of programs and projects that may be found in other states.

For information on programs in your state, a search using your favorite search engine, such as Google, AOL, Yahoo, MSN, or any of the many others, and using a phrase such as "('your state') volunteer program" should get you on the right track.

Budgetary Problems

As the Federal and state governments attempt to deal with budget problems, much of the funding for seniors' programs is being curtailed. This is an opportunity for creative retirees to find ways to meet the objectives of the various programs at lower, or no, cost to the taxpayers.

1

Peace Corps

Peace Corps
111 20th Street
NW
Washington, DC
20526
(800) 424-8580
peacecorps.gov

The Peace Corps is an independent agency within the executive branch of the United States government. Over 400 older Americans currently serve as Peace Corps volunteers around the world, many as married couples. Individuals work in many skill areas, but are primarily involved with education and business.

There are currently eleven Peace Corps regional recruiting offices throughout the U.S.

The President of the United States appoints the Peace Corps Director and Deputy Director, and the appointments must be confirmed by the U.S. Senate. The Senate Foreign Relations Committee is charged with general oversight of the activities and programs of the Peace Corps, and the House Committee on International Relations serves a similar function.

The Peace Corps' annual budget is determined each year by the congressional budget and appropriations process, and is part of the foreign operations budget. The Peace Corps' annual budget for fiscal year 2003 was $295 million.

President Bush has devoted the highest level of funding to the Peace Corps than at any time in the history of the agency. Generally, the Peace Corps budget is about one percent of the foreign operations budget.

The Peace Corps recently ran a classified ad in the Wall Street Journal for Country Directors, indicating that there are current opportunities for those with "senior level executive experience."

SCORE
409 Third Street
 SW, 6th Floor
Washington DC
 20024
(800) 634-0245
score.org

2

SCORE

The Service Corps of

Retired Executives

SCORE is a way for retirees with business management experience to assist entrepreneurs and small businesses throughout the U.S.

The SCORE Association, headquartered in Washington, DC, is a nonprofit association dedicated to entrepreneurial education and the formation, growth and success of small businesses nationwide. 10,500 retired and working volunteers provide free business counseling and advice as a public service. SCORE offers 'Ask SCORE' email advice online.

A resource partner with the Small Business Administration, SCORE volunteers serve as "Counselors to America's Small Business." Local chapters provide free counseling and low-cost workshops in their communities. SCORE assists approximately 300,000 entrepreneurs annually.

Working with 389 local chapters, SCORE reaches small business owners across the Country—from Maine to Hawaii. SCORE chapters serve as a local connection to small business know-how. Through free, small business counseling and support services, SCORE volunteers help keep businesses going and growing.

3

Citizen Corps

Citizen Corps is an opportunity for retirees to serve their communities in areas including crime prevention and emergency response, particularly in connection with FEMA.

Citizen Corps, a vital component of USA Freedom Corps, was created to help coordinate volunteer activities that will make our communities safer, stronger, and better prepared to respond to any emergency situation. It provides opportunities for people to participate in a range of measures to make their families, their homes, and their communities safer from the threats of crime, terrorism, and disasters of all kinds.

Citizen Corps programs build on the successful efforts that are in place in many communities around the Country to prevent crime and respond to emergencies. Programs that started through local innovation are the foundation for Citizen Corps and this national approach to citizen participation in community safety.

Citizen Corps is coordinated nationally by the Federal Emergency Management Agency. In this capacity, FEMA works closely with other Federal entities, state and local governments, first responders and emergency managers, the volunteer community, and the White House Office of the USA Freedom Corps.

Citizen Corps programs include: Neighborhood Watch, Volunteers in Police Service, Medical Reserve Corps, and Citizen Corps Councils.

Fire Corps
1050 17th Street
 NW, Suite 490
Washington, DC
 20036
(202) 887-4809
firecorps.org

4

Fire Corps

A new USA Freedom Corps initiative provides opportunities to work as a volunteer to help your local fire department.

Fire Corps is a recent Citizen Corps (part of USA Freedom Corps) initiative to support fire departments throughout the Country. It is a partnership among the National Volunteer Fire Council, the International Association of Fire Chiefs Volunteer Combination & Officers Section, and the International Association of Fire Fighters.

The mission of Fire Corps is to enhance the ability of fire departments to utilize citizen advocates and provide individuals with opportunities to support their local fire departments with their time and talent.

Its goal is to support and supplement volunteer, combination, and career fire departments through the use of citizen advocates for non-operational related activities.

Fire service input to the program is provided through the Fire Corps National Advisory Committee, which gives strategic direction and important feedback from the field to Fire Corps.

The program was launched in December of 2004, so many local fire departments have yet to become involved with the program. For information on how you can become involved, and help your local fire department become participants, contact the website above.

5

RSVP

Retired and Senior
Volunteer Program

**Retired and Senior
Volunteer Program**
The Corporation for
National Service
1201 New York
Avenue NW
Washington, DC 20525
(202) 606-5000
seniorcorps.org

*RSVP volunteers work in their communities in areas such as mentoring,
teaching English as a second language and teaching business skills.*

The Retired and Senior Volunteer Program (RSVP) is a project of the Senior Corps
program. Volunteers serve in a diverse range of nonprofit organizations, public
agencies, and faith-based groups.

Among other activities, they mentor at-risk youth, organize Neighborhood
Watch programs, test drinking water for contaminants, teach English to immi-
grants, and lend their business skills to community groups that provide critical
social services. Approximately 500,000 volunteers serve an average of four
hours a week at an estimated 65,000 local organizations.

RSVP is open to people age fifty-five and over. Local organizations, both public and private, receive grants to sponsor and operate RSVP projects in their community. These projects recruit seniors to serve from a few hours a month to
almost full-time, though the average commitment is four hours a week.

Most volunteers are paired with local community and faith-based organizations that are already helping to meet community needs. RSVP volunteers are
not paid, but sponsoring organizations may reimburse them for some costs
incurred during service.

RSVP provides appropriate volunteer insurance coverage, and volunteers
receive pre-service orientation and in-service training from the agency or organization where they are placed.

Volunteers for Prosperity
USA Freedom Corps
1600 Pennsylvania
 Avenue NW
Washington, DC 20500
volunteersforprosperity.
 com

6

Volunteers for Prosperity

An opportunity for skilled retirees to work in a variety of countries under the auspices of the U.S. Agency for International Development. Assignments range from a few weeks to several months.

Volunteers for Prosperity is a volunteer-based initiative designed to support major U.S. development objectives overseas, using the talents of highly skilled Americans who work with U.S. organizations helping to promote health and generate prosperity in countries around the world. It is a Presidential initiative of the USA Freedom Corps.

President Bush launched the Volunteers for Prosperity initiative to allow those individuals with skills in such areas as health care, information technology, financial services, trade and investment, education, and agricultural development, answer the call to service and help meet global needs.

Coordinated and administered by the U.S. Agency for International Development (USAID), Federal departments and agencies overseeing major U.S. development initiatives in countries abroad will seek ways to expand and enhance volunteer service opportunities for international development activities.

As part of Volunteers for Prosperity, the USA Freedom Corps will match doctors, nurses, teachers, engineers, economists, computer specialists, and others with U.S. organizations working on specific U.S. development initiatives including: the Emergency Plan for AIDS Relief; the Trade for Africa Development and Enterprise Initiative; the Water for the Poor Initiative; the Digital Freedom Initiative; the Middle East Partnership Initiative and the Millennium Challenge Corporation.

7

California
Service Corps

*The California Service Corps is a California program that has counterparts
in most of the other states. Its community service activities are funded
by a variety of Federal programs.*

The California Service Corps, formally GO SERV, is California's national service commission, charged with administering AmeriCorps, Citizen Corps, and Cesar Chavez Day of Service and Learning in California, and promoting service and volunteerism statewide. Its mission is to bring Californians together to meet community challenges through service and volunteerism.

Today there is a growing field of opportunities in California for people of all ages to become involved in their communities through nonprofits, schools, colleges and universities, and places of worship and employment. Whether you're looking for your first service opportunity or for more meaningful ways to serve, their website can help you.

CSC's role includes calling on Californians to become involved in their communities and challenge institutions to create and support service and volunteer opportunities, connecting people to service and volunteer opportunities in their communities, and planning for and building a comprehensive and integrated service and volunteerism system throughout California.

The CSC website, a database of volunteer and service opportunities addressing a variety of community issues, can help you find a volunteer opportunity in your community.

**United States Coast
Guard Auxiliary
Center**
9449 Watson Industrial
 Park
St. Louis, MO 63126
(800) 368-5647
cgaux.org

8

U.S. Coast
Guard Auxiliary

If you enjoy and are experienced in boating or flying, the U.S. Coast Guard can use your services. You can assist in patrolling our waterways, assist in training and monitoring the boating public and serve side by side with active duty members of the Coast Guard team at their stations and in times of disaster.

The U.S. Coast Guard Auxiliary is the civilian, non-military component of the Coast Guard, created by an act of Congress in 1939. The Auxiliary directly supports the Coast Guard in all of its missions except military and law enforcement actions.

Recreational boating in the U.S. is growing rapidly. To help make boating safer for all, the Auxiliary needs more qualified members. Members receive the world's finest on-the-water training. Advanced training courses in navigation, seamanship, communications, weather, patrols, administration and search and rescue are available, as well as courses from the Coast Guard Institute.

The Auxiliary is the only volunteer organization within the Department of Homeland Security. Its maritime public security and safety responsibilities expanded greatly after 9/11. It helps safeguard the lives of United States citizens. With the increasing threats to American security and interests, the challenges of supporting the Auxiliary have grown.

In addition to boating activities, many Auxiliarists are pilots, and have flown over 10,000 hours of air patrols. The Auxiliary receives no direct funding from the Federal government and volunteer Auxiliarists serve without compensation.

Volunteer Opportunities

*V*olunteering is certainly the most available activity for those who want to do something for society. There are thousands of organizations looking for free talent, from needy neighbors or relatives to your local church and charitable groups to national and international organizations and causes.

An important issue is whether the individual can get satisfaction and fulfillment from the activity and its impact on society.

The following pages describe organizations that can lead to specific opportunities and in the process give you some idea of what the organizations do and the best way to contact them. They are a good way to get ideas of the range of activities and opportunities that are close to where you live and that appeal to your sense of purpose.

There are many opportunities to serve. As you consider these various ideas, ask yourself what kind of a role you think you might want. Do you want to take on a regular commitment, or would you rather work on a project basis, when you feel like working and when there is a specific task that can use your talents and give you a sense of fulfillment?

Do you want to work directly with the individuals needing the help, or would you rather work in a management or planning capacity, or coming up with new programs? How much time do you want to commit? You can work locally or travel to other parts of the Country or world.

Other things to consider are your reasons for wanting to volunteer, the types of activities or projects you might be interested in, what your strengths or weaknesses are. What do you enjoy doing? Do you want to work in a small organization, or one that operates on a larger scale?

These suggestions and considerations apply not only to the process of volunteering, but to the many other categories and ideas presented in this guidebook.

There are many volunteering opportunities both here and abroad. Because the opportunities are numerous, and the commitments quite different between domestic activities and those overseas, we have presented the suggestions in two sections: Volunteering—U.S. and Volunteering—International.

Volunteering—U.S.

Volunteering close to home is easy to get into. We are all aware of many opportunities through our churches and community organizations.

The following are representative organizations with broad scope. They can help you focus on opportunities of special interest to you. Some of these groups will lead you to many other opportunities. Others may serve as catalysts for you to consider in dealing with organizations or needs that may be familiar to you, or that you may already be involved with.

AARP
601 E Street NW
Washington, DC
20049
(800) 424-3410
aarp.org

9

AARP

American Association
of Retired Persons

AARP is the 800-pound gorilla in the field of retirement. If you haven't heard from AARP, you are under fifty-five. They offer a number of ideas and services related to volunteering.

AARP, the nation's largest retirement organization, offers a broad range of products and services related to retirement and aging. If you are over fifty-five and not already a member, you will want to join. Membership is quite inexpensive and provides valuable information and contacts.

AARP operates numerous volunteer, service, and employment programs, including Connections for Independent Living, The Volunteer Talent Bank, and the Experience Corps for Independent Living. In addition to these programs, AARP offers the following comments on the volunteer process:

"At different points in your life, you may be ready to do some volunteer work. You may see it as a chance to give back to your community, to support a cause that you believe in, to develop new skills, or to establish new friendships. Whatever your reason, you can put your time and talents to good use by volunteering in your community.

"Your help is always needed. Many organizations are facing shortages of volunteers while the demand for direct services continues to grow. To help organizations keep up with increasing demands, volunteers now play a greater role in developing and providing key services. Today's volunteers bring a breadth of skills and experiences to many organizations. Behind the scenes and in the forefront, you too can make a difference in the lives of others in your community."

American Red Cross National Headquarters
2025 E Street NW
Washington, DC
 20006
(202) 303-4498
redcross.volunteer
 match.org

10

American Red Cross

The Red Cross is everywhere, thanks to the many volunteers who offer their time to help in the many services the organization provides.

Each year over one million Americans serve as Red Cross volunteers serving local community needs—helping people in emergencies, providing half the Nation's blood supply, teaching first aid and CPR courses, delivering emergency messages to members of the military, organizing programs for the elderly, etc.

Red Cross volunteers work directly with people, serve on boards of directors, serve as managers, advisors, and provide behind the scenes support.

Be a Red Cross volunteer. Helping others feels good, and helps you feel good about yourself. Your local Red Cross can work with you to provide rewarding experiences, opportunities to utilize your talents, or provide training to help you serve your community.

To find volunteer opportunities with the Red Cross, you can review current volunteer opportunities in over 100 communities listed at their Volunteer Match website or review current volunteer opportunities at the American Red Cross national headquarters.

11

Habitat For Humanity

Habitat for Humanity International
121 Habitat Street
Americus, GA 31709-3498
(912) 924-6935
habitat.org

If you like to use your skills with a hammer and saw, or want to learn how to wire a kitchen, Habitat is a place to check out.

Habitat is a nonprofit, ecumenical Christian housing ministry dedicated to eliminating substandard housing and homelessness. It has been made famous by the involvement of former President Jimmy Carter as an active participant in its program.

Since 1976, Habitat has built more than 50,000 houses with families throughout the United States and another 100,000-plus houses in communities around the world. Now at work in ninety-two countries, they are building a house every twenty-six minutes. By 2005, Habitat houses will be sheltering one million people.

Habitat invites people from all faiths and walks of life to work together in partnership, building houses with families in need. A significant portion of its short- and long-term volunteers are older adults. They welcome all people to join them as they build simple, decent, affordable houses in partnership with those who lack adequate shelter.

12

Executive Service Corps

Assisting various nonprofit organizations throughout the U.S. to improve their operational and fund-raising effectiveness is the basic role of ESC.

The Executive Service Corps is a nonprofit organization helping other nonprofit organizations to survive and thrive through consulting and coaching services provided by volunteer retired or semi-retired executives and professionals from the corporate, public and nonprofit sectors.

Since 1977, ESC has applied proven business planning and management skills to the nonprofit sector. Their consultants are men and women who have held highly responsible positions in business, the professions and nonprofit enterprises. They have entered the "give-back" phase of their careers and volunteer their time, energy and vast experience to help strengthen nonprofit organizations.

The volunteer consultants work in their areas of expertise: planning, marketing, public relations, finance, human resources, information technology, general management, leadership, and areas specific to nonprofit organizations such as fund-raising and board development.

Consultants find the experience personally rewarding because they stay involved in challenging work, experience on-going training to enhance their consulting work and have the opportunity to develop new relationships with other consultants and members of the community.

The Executive Service Corps currently operates in twenty-seven states and the District of Columbia. Each network office has its own specialties and programs. Contact the ESC nearest you for further information.

13

1-800 VOLUNTEER

*If you are looking for exposure to a wide variety of volunteer
opportunities to consider, this is a great place to start.*

1-800 VOLUNTEER is a web-based volunteer recruitment, referral, and tracking resource. It is managed by local volunteer centers within their communities.

It provides volunteers with a direct connection to local volunteer opportunities that match interests, skills, and the common desire to make a difference.

The individual volunteer centers make this resource available to the community so that volunteers have easy access to numerous quality, varied, and current volunteer opportunities.

Also, nonprofit organizations are able to further promote their mission and their organization, as well as recruit, place, and track their volunteers.

1-800 VOLUNTEER is a service of the Points of Light Foundation and the Volunteer Center National Network.

**Environmental
Alliance for
Senior Involve-
ment**
8733 Old
 Dumphries Road
Catlett, VA 20119
(540) 788-3274
easi.org

14

Environmental Alliance
for Senior Involvement

*Through the EASI, AARP and the U.S. EPA have joined forces to provide
opportunities for retirees to assist with environmental related programs.*

The Environmental Alliance for Senior Involvement (EASI) is a national nonprofit
coalition of environmental, aging and volunteer organizations established in 1991
as the result of an agreement between the U.S. Environmental Protection Agency
and AARP.

EASI's partners include over 300 national, state and local public and private
organizations. Over 100,000 seniors are involved in significant environmental
activities through the Senior Environment Corps programs established by EASI with
local state partners.

EASI identifies support for senior volunteer activities that address national, state
and local environmental priorities. Through its national network of 12,000 local
organizations, EASI selects local hosts to recruit, train and recognize senior volunteers who carry out a wide range of environmental activities.

EASI is headquartered in Catlett, Virginia and has offices in Arlington, Virginia;
Washington, DC; Red Lion, Pennsylvania; and Denton, Texas. Its staff oversees government and private sector funding that is granted to local host organizations, providing support for recruitment, training, and supplying senior environmental
volunteer programs.

Current programs include: Water Quality Monitoring, Watershed Assessment,
Children's Health Initiative, Classroom Environmental Education, Forest Manage-
ment, Outdoor Environmental Education, Stream Corridor Restoration, Brownfields
Revitalization, Source Water/Groundwater Protection, Home Testing for Radon, Pol-
lution Prevention Technical Assistance, Community Gardens, Senior Ranger Corps,
EASI Ambassadors, Partners Against Weeds, and Senior Volunteer Leadership.

15

Volunteers of America

**Volunteers of
America
National Office**
1660 Duke Street
Alexandria, VA
22314-3421
(800) 899-0089
voa.org

*VOA has programs nationally that involve retirees in solutions
to community needs.*

Volunteers of America is a national, nonprofit, spiritually based organization providing local human service programs and opportunities for individual and community involvement.

From rural America to inner-city neighborhoods, Volunteers of America provides outreach programs that deal with today's most pressing social needs. The organization helps youths at risk, frail elderly, abused and neglected children, people with disabilities, homeless individuals and many others.

Almost a third of its more than 40,000 volunteers are seniors, about double that of five years ago.

Many of the VOA local programs are in need of volunteers. Find out where your nearest local office is located and how to contact them. Their national office is located in the Washington, DC area.

**National
Retiree Volun-
teer Coalition**
4915 West 35th
  Street, Suite 205
Minneapolis, MN
  55416
(888) 733-NRVC
nrvc.org

16

National Retiree
Volunteer Coalition

*The NRVC assists corporations develop ways to keep their retirees
involved and active in community volunteer programs.*

Associated with the Volunteers of America, the NRVC is a nonprofit consulting organization dedicated to creating corporate retiree programs, through which retirees can serve with former work colleagues under the banner of their former employer.

Projects include volunteering in the areas of education, community revitalization, environmental concerns, and public health.

NRVC is a resource for forming strong partnerships among retirees, their former employers and their communities.

The organization offers consultation, program development and training to corporations, universities, healthcare systems, governmental institutions and any other employer interested in innovative, expansive retiree volunteer programs.

To learn more about NRVC and how you or your organization can become involved today, contact their national office.

17

VolunteerMatch

VolunteerMatch
385 Grove Street
San Francisco, CA
94102
(415) 241-6868
volunteermatch.org

Another important resource for getting retirees together with opportunities to serve in thousands of different ways.

VolunteerMatch is a nonprofit, online service that helps interested volunteers get involved with community service organizations throughout the United States.

Volunteers enter their zip code on the VolunteerMatch website to quickly find local volunteer opportunities matching individual interests and schedules. This simple, effective service has generated hundreds of thousands of volunteer referrals nationwide.

VolunteerMatch is the recipient of two 2001 Webby Awards for "Activism" and "Services", has been honored by the Smithsonian Institution and MIT, and has been recognized for its social service efforts. A recent search indicated that they had over 39,000 volunteering opportunities available.

A search by zip code for opportunities within twenty miles turned up 441 opportunities in the Los Angeles area. Of these, eighty-two were categorized as being those seeking seniors as volunteers.

They also have a section called "Virtual Volunteering." where you can help out by using your computer and the Internet.

Points of Light Foundation
1400 I Street NW
  Suite 800
Washington, DC
  20005
(800) Volunteer
pointsoflight.org

18

Points of Light Foundation

This foundation does not directly mobilize or coordinate specific volunteer initiatives within local communities. It is a source of perspective on various programs nationally as it provides support to volunteer centers and other agencies that are responsible for coordinating volunteers.

The Points of Light Foundation's research and evaluation activities seek to build a bridge between volunteer management practitioners and the academic community to increase knowledge of volunteering and its effects on social problems. With the Volunteer Center National Network, it engages and mobilizes millions of volunteers who are helping to solve serious social problems in thousands of communities.

Through a variety of programs and services, the Foundation encourages people from all walks of life—businesses, nonprofits, faith-based organizations, low-income communities, families, youth, and older adults—to volunteer.

Based in Washington, DC, the Foundation advocates community service through its partnership with the Volunteer Center National Network. Together, they reach millions of people in thousands of communities to help mobilize people and resources, to deliver solutions that address community problems.

Across the Country, innovative age fifty-plus volunteer projects are beginning to reshape civil society. Today's older adults are redefining a new stage of life to reflect the health, vitality, and possibilities ahead. Innovative volunteer projects that leverage their experience, skills, and freedom, provide fifty-plus adults challenging and rewarding opportunities.

Volunteer America
PO Box 847
Minden, NV 89423
volunteeramerica.net

19

Volunteer America

*Preservation and protection of the Nation's public lands
is the focus of Volunteer America.*

Not to be confused with Volunteers of America, Volunteer America connects individuals, families and groups with volunteer opportunities and volunteer vacations on public lands all across America.

Volunteering is an American tradition that over the years has made an immeasurable contribution to communities, organizations and individuals throughout the Country. Volunteer opportunities exist among all public land management agencies as well as with nonprofit organizations that provide services on public lands.

Volunteer programs have something for almost everyone—retirees, professionals, homemakers, students and young people, as well as service clubs and organizations. If you like people and care about our Country's natural resources, then public agencies and service organizations can use your time and talents.

Some volunteers work full-time for several months, while others donate a few hours a day each week, or contribute a one-time service. Students may volunteer to earn college credits through an approved intern program, or to become familiar with an agency's or organization's activities and philosophy.

Many individuals have found that their volunteer experience has guided them towards job interests and possible careers. Retirees or others with skills to share often find that a volunteer position provides them with a favorable change of pace.

Depending on the nature of the volunteer project and the availability of funds, some volunteer positions provide items such as housing, a uniform, a subsistence allowance, and work related transportation.

**Princeton
Project 55**
12 Stockton
  Street
Princeton, NJ
  08540
(609) 921-8808
project55.org

20

Princeton Project 55

*This is an example of one graduating class of one university making an effort
to involve its members in service to society over the years since graduation.*

Princeton Project 55 is a non-partisan, nonprofit organization established by the Class of 1955 at Princeton. It was born of the realization that there was a vast untapped resource, available for the public good, among groups of college alumni.

It continues to be involved in mentoring, service exchange, and character education programs in several areas of the Country.

It also works with other classes of Princeton alumni and with alumni groups from other universities such as Bucknell, Dartmouth, Moravian, Smith, and Williams.

Princeton Project 55 is a possible model for other schools and their alumni who may want to develop similar programs.

**Congress of
California Seniors**
1228 N Street, #30
Sacramento, CA 95814
(800) 543-3352
seniors.org

21

Congress of
California Seniors

*One state's program to involve volunteers in a variety of ways
to assist other seniors.*

The Congress of California Seniors (CCS), established in 1977, is a statewide nonprofit education and advocacy organization dedicated to improving the life of seniors and their families. Through its educational program and legislative action, CCS has emerged as a major progressive force for California's seniors.

The Congress of California Seniors provides access to many opportunities to volunteer time and energies in one or more of the activities and educational outreach programs conducted throughout the State.

Most of the statewide legislative activities are conducted from the Sacramento office, with occasional hearings and demonstrations organized from the Los Angeles office. Individuals interested in participating in these activities are encouraged to join CCS.

In addition to statewide activities, CCS is divided into regions throughout the State. Each region has a regional chairperson. The Sacramento office will put you in touch with the regional chairperson in your area. Other states have similar programs.

Volunteering—International

The following ideas will provide a broad range of opportunities to combine volunteering with international travel and involvement.

One of the things that the reader must consider is that many of these opportunities involve payment by the volunteer for that opportunity. The fees may be expenses alone—travel, housing, food, etc.—or might include fees to the organizing group.

This does not necessarily condemn the activity; it just suggests that you should know what you are getting into.

Another consideration is that with budget cuts, some of the volunteer programs that have been subsidized by government agencies may have less capacity to use volunteer help. It may be more difficult to get involved unless you have very specifically needed experience and skills.

Another variable is the amount of time involved. Some of these situations involve a short commitment, one or two weeks, while others are much longer.

22

International Executive Service Corps

International Executive Service Corps
901 15th Street NW, Suite 350
Washington, DC 20005
(202) 326-0280
iesc.org

IESC provides opportunities for volunteers to work with businesses all over the world to help improve their business management and promotional capabilities.

The International Executive Service Corps is the largest not-for-profit business development organization of its kind in the world. It has been working since 1964 to increase the competitiveness of entrepreneurs and small and medium-sized firms in the developing world.

The IESC expertise also extends to strengthening non-governmental and business support organizations. The public administration program engenders strong democratic practices, values and institutions among the new, emerging democracies.

Volunteers serve as American ambassadors of good will, transferring knowledge and expertise to create sustainable development. By helping people in the less developed world improve their lives, they ensure that globalization is truly global.

IESC's services include: access to global markets, strategic alliance matchmaking, import and export promotion, managerial and technical assistance, market research studies, equipment and technology sourcing, business planning, pre-investment screening, post-investment assistance, and access to financing.

IESC volunteer experts transfer their knowledge and skills to assist entrepreneurs, small and medium-sized businesses, business support organizations, government agencies and non-governmental organizations.

**International
Volunteer Programs
Association**
PO Box 18
Presque Isle, MI 49777
(734) 528-2496
volunteerinternational.org

23

International Volunteer Programs

The International Volunteer Programs Association coordinates international opportunities for a large number of member organizations involved in volunteer and exchange programs.

IVPA is an alliance of nonprofit, non-governmental organizations based in the Americas that are involved in international volunteer and internship exchanges. The organization encourages excellence and responsibility in the field of international volunteerism and promotes public awareness of, and greater access to international volunteer programs.

The IVPA website provides an excellent overview of the international volunteering process, with the pros and cons of each activity, what to expect, and leads to various organizations offering opportunities.

Any program that regularly sends groups or individuals to work abroad as volunteers, interns or lay missionaries, for any length of time, falls under the broad category of "International Volunteer Programs."

International volunteer programs offer hands-on learning experiences which promote cross-cultural understanding, cooperation, and solidarity among individuals and communities around the world.

IVPA cannot guarantee the quality of programs operated by its member organizations, but it does strive to collaborate to ensure the highest quality within the field of international volunteerism.

24

Cross-Cultural Solutions

Cross-Cultural Solutions
2 Clinton Place
New Rochelle, NY
10801
(800) 380-4777
crossculturalsolutions.org

Offering volunteer and insight programs throughout the world, Cross-Cultural Solutions is a fee based service providing opportunities to work in humanitarian programs.

Cross-Cultural Solutions is active in the international volunteer field, sending thousands of volunteers overseas every year. They are in Special Consultative Status with the United Nations Economic and Social Council and in partnership with CARE, one of the world's largest international humanitarian organizations.

CCS was directly involved in coordinating volunteers for the World Trade Center relief efforts after September 11, 2001. Founded in 1995, Cross-Cultural Solutions is headquartered in New Rochelle, New York, with an office in Brighton, United Kingdom.

The organization operates eighteen programs out of eleven countries, with more than 250 staff members in fifteen offices worldwide. To date, the organization has brought more than 7,000 participants to countries around the world.

They offer two types of programs, Volunteer and Insight. The Volunteer Programs, which focus on cultural immersion through volunteering and cultural learning opportunities, are year-round, and normally range from two to twelve weeks.

The Insight programs are shorter, typically one week, in which participants are given the opportunity to travel deep into the heart of a community and join in their daily life. They get to work on local service projects in a fascinating part of the world, and experience another culture.

CCS has programs in Brazil, China, Costa Rica, Ghana, Guatemala, India, Peru, Russia, Tanzania, and Thailand. There are fees to the volunteers; the fee charged for these programs average about $1,000 per week, plus the cost of transportation to the site.

Action Without Borders, Inc.
79 Fifth Avenue, 17th floor
New York, NY 10003
(212) 843-3973
idealist.org

25

Action Without Borders
Idea List

An opportunity to search a huge database of organizations around the world to find volunteer opportunities.

First called the Contact Center Network, Action Without Borders was founded in 1995 to build a network of neighborhood Contact Centers that would provide a one-stop shop for volunteer opportunities and nonprofit services in communities around the world.

Idea List is a project of Action Without Borders. Over 37,000 nonprofit and community organizations in 165 countries can be searched by name, location or mission. In the Idea List website you can find volunteer opportunities in your community and around the world, and a list of organizations that can help you volunteer abroad.

You can define what information you would like to receive by email from among the job openings, volunteer opportunities, internships, events, and resources posted by organizations all over the world.

You can design your own volunteer opportunity by setting up one or more Volunteer Profiles with your interests, skills and schedule.

These profiles can then be searched by organizations in Idea List.

26

Global Crossroad

Global Crossroad
8772 Quarters Lake
Road, Suite 9
Baton Rouge, LA
70809
(800) 413-2008
globalcrossroad.com

Global Crossroad is a lower cost way to get involved with volunteer opportunities abroad, providing links to groups in a variety of countries.

Global Crossroad is a fast-growing organization that coordinates volunteer, internship, and mini-adventure opportunities worldwide.

Based in the United States, Global Crossroad is highly affordable in comparison with similar organizations based in the UK.

The organization offers many exciting volunteering opportunities to international volunteers in countries such as India, Nepal, China, Sri Lanka, Thailand, Mongolia, Ghana, Cambodia and Costa Rica.

Their unique and stimulating programs engage volunteers in breathtaking journey. Global Crossroad welcomes people of all ages between eighteen and seventy years old, who are capable of working as volunteers.

Global Crossroad invites you to join this extraordinary adventure and embark on the journey of a lifetime.

InterAction
1717 Massachusetts
 Ave. NW, Suite 701
Washington, DC
 20036
(202) 667-8227
interaction.org

27

InterAction

InterAction is a coordinator of many different organizations working throughout the world on problems of economic and social development.

InterAction is the largest alliance of U.S.-based international development and humanitarian nongovernmental organizations. With more than 160 members operating in every developing country, they work to overcome poverty, exclusion and suffering by advancing social justice and basic dignity for all.

Formed in 1984, and based in Washington, DC with a staff of thirty-five, InterAction includes members headquartered in twenty-five states. The organization convenes and coordinates its members so in unison they can influence policy and debate on issues affecting tens of millions of people worldwide and improve their own practices.

Both faith-based and secular, these organizations foster economic and social development; provide relief to those affected by disaster and war; assist refugees and internally displaced persons; advance human rights; support gender equality; protect the environment; address population concerns; and press for more equitable, just, and effective public policies.

InterAction can provide information on its various member organizations and the types of volunteer support they might seek.

28

NetHope

If you have skills related to communications or information technology systems or applications, there may be an opportunity to help under-developed sectors of the world market.

NetHope is a global network of leading international nonprofit organizations in development, relief and conservation, working to better leverage technology for the benefit of the poorest people in the world.

Its member organizations include: Save the Children, ActionAid, Habitat for Humanity, CARE, World Vision, Mercy Corps, Children International, Winrock International, Oxfam International, the Nature Conservancy, Christian Children's Fund, Catholic Relief Services, International Rescue Committee, Plan International, and Relief International.

Corporate supporters include Cisco Systems, Microsoft, Inmarsat, Eutelsat, Accenture, McKinsey & Company, Baker and McKenzie, and others.

NetHope member non-governmental organizations are committed to and experienced in leveraging information technology and the Internet to support their missions. They collaborate in applying information and communication technology to improve their educational, healthcare, environmental and relief services in support of the world's neediest.

The vision is improving the lives of the most underserved people in the developing world through access to information and communications over the Internet. NetHope's mission is to build relationships, collaboration, and knowledge sharing in the nonprofit sector around information and communication technology, resulting in communications infrastructure and access to information that improves the lives of the world's most disadvantaged, vulnerable and poorest people.

For interested individuals or organizations, there are from time to time opportunities for technical and project management expertise on volunteer or contract basis. And there is always a need for funding for working capital and projects.

Global Volunteers
75 East Little Canada
  Road
St. Paul, MN
  55117-1628
(800) 487-1074
globalvolunteers.org

29

Global Volunteers

Global Volunteers offers the opportunity for "volunteer vacations," short term service assignments in nineteen countries on six continents.

In 1984, Global Volunteers laid the foundation for what became known a decade later as "volunteer vacations," short-term service opportunities on community development programs in host communities abroad. Today, as a non-sectarian organization offering volunteer vacations worldwide, Global Volunteers mobilizes some 150 service-learning teams year around to work in nineteen countries on six continents.

As a non-governmental organization in special consultative status with the United Nations, Global Volunteers is uniquely positioned to represent local leaders in an international arena, and to engage short term volunteers in local development efforts with long-lasting results.

At the request of local leaders and indigenous host organizations, Global Volunteers mobilizes teams of volunteers to live and work with local people on human and economic development projects identified by the community as important to its long-term development.

30

World Vision

World Vision
P.O. Box 9716
Federal Way, WA
98063-9716
(888) 511-6598
worldvision.org

World Vision is a religious organization working with poor children and families in nearly 100 countries, including the United States.

Founded in 1950, World Vision is a Christian humanitarian organization serving the world's poorest children and families.

World Vision was started to help children orphaned in the Korean War. The organization has grown well beyond its child-assistance roots to facilitating the transformation of entire communities with water programs, health care education, agricultural and economic development, and strategic Christian leadership activities.

Through sponsorship, World Vision assists children in struggling communities with food, education, health care, and vocational training, supported by monthly contributions from donors. As children began to flourish through sponsorship in Korea, the program expanded into other Asian countries and eventually into Latin America and Africa.

World Vision extends assistance to all people, regardless of their religious beliefs, gender, race, or ethnic background.

Relationships are the starting point and the end goal of World Vision's work. Through relationships with community leaders, World Vision's staff helps communities set goals that families can achieve by working together.

Mentoring, Helping Kids

The following Idea pages provide information on specific programs and on groups that can provide further contacts related to mentoring. They also include other opportunities to work with and help children that might not necessarily be considered 'mentoring.'

Mentoring is probably one of the more satisfying activities for experienced seniors. By carefully selecting the activity, retirees can find ways to use their own special knowledge, experience and interests. Opportunities range from existing programs to those you may create based on your own background and the individuals with whom you come into contact.

Mentoring is one of the easiest activities in which to get involved, from working one-on-one with individuals you may know, to working with local community organizations or schools, to national groups. It is the broadest in terms of the type and ages of individuals with whom you can relate.

You may mentor children, high school students, college students, young graduates starting in their careers, people in their mid-stage career development, business persons needing help, retirees or any number of other special need situations. The range of topics is limitless; constrained only by your own interests, skills and experiences and the interests and needs of your student. Mentoring may be the best use of your life's experiences.

Other ideas in this section are related to helping kids in other than a mentoring capacity. Although once you are involved with a kid, or group of kids, in need, you may very well become a mentor.

31

National Mentoring Partnership

National Mentoring Partnership
1600 Duke Street, Suite 300
Alexandria, VA 22314
(703) 224-2200
mentoring.org

A resource group for mentoring programs, the National Mentoring Partnership provides access to all types of opportunities nationwide and internationally.

The National Mentoring Partnership is an advocate for the expansion of mentoring and a resource for mentors and mentoring initiatives nationwide. Mentoring programs around the Country rely on the organization for cutting-edge products and services to help them grow their programs.

Through the National Mentoring Institute, local, national and international organizations offer solutions that are both cost-effective and easy to access: including online training and recruitment, e-mentoring standards, tool kits and counseling from experts. It assists providers in operating effective programs, helps them identify problems and find resources.

If you manage or work for an existing mentoring program, their Run a Program service will help you: network with other providers who are operating mentoring programs similar to yours; find mentoring programs, products, experts, and research that will help you meet your program's unique needs; determine best practices for building a sound mentoring program; and pinpoint underlying (and often hidden) problems within your mentoring program that may block your effectiveness.

32

National
Mentoring Center

*The National Mentoring Center is focused on complex youth
development programs, providing training and technical assistance.*

The National Mentoring Center is a project of the Northwest Regional Educational Laboratory, based in Portland, Oregon. The NMC is one of the preeminent national training and technical assistance providers for mentoring programs across the United States.

Created and funded primarily by the Office of Juvenile Justice and Delinquency Prevention (OJJDP), the National Mentoring Center provides a range of services related to mentoring. It is staffed by a team of professionals with diverse and complementary skill-sets.

Collectively, the NMC staff has extensive expertise in the planning, development, implementation, and evaluation of complex youth development projects and intensive training and technical assistance services.

By working as an intermediary between funding agencies and local programs, the primary goal of the NMC is to improve the quality and safety of mentoring programs. By strengthening program practices, they help to improve the positive outcomes for youth at the program level.

The National Mentoring Center offers hands-on training through a variety of conferences and other events.

**Neighboring
Points of Light
Foundation**
pointsoflight.org/
programs/
neighboring

33

Neighborhood Transformation

The Points of Light Foundation, working in partnership with The Annie E. Casey Foundation, invites you to embrace neighboring as a way to strengthen families and transform America's toughest communities.

In 1996, The Annie E. Casey Foundation challenged the Points of Light Foundation to expand its understanding of volunteering and explore the role it plays in transforming 'tough' neighborhoods into connected and family supportive places.

The Points of Light Foundation utilized the opportunity to listen, learn, and share their discoveries. The neighboring model is an empowerment and assessment-based approach to volunteer engagement in under-resourced communities. The two organizations invite you to be a partner in bringing neighboring to America's under-resourced communities to create family-supportive neighborhoods.

By dedicating financial and human resources to support and foster local efforts, you can be a partner to strengthen families and transform neighborhoods. For many families living in tough communities, the gaps in critical connections are widening. That's why volunteering and neighboring have never been more important than they are today.

Organizations and individuals working in tough communities need to see community members not just as recipients of services but as change agents and equal partners. Promoting real community self-reliance is a clear objective of any initiative to enrich opportunities for residents.

**Court Appointed
Special Advocates**
1615 E. 17th Street,
Suite 100
Santa Ana, CA
(714) 619-5155
casaoc.org

34

Court Appointed
Special Advocates

*The Court Appointed Special Advocates program mentors and
advocates for abused, abandoned and neglected children.*

Founded in 1985, with major support from the Junior League of Orange County,
California, Court Appointed Special Advocates (CASA) of Orange County is one of
more than 900 CASA programs nationwide dedicated to providing quality interven-
tion and advocacy services for abused, abandoned, and neglected children.

Based on a model originated by Judge David Soukup of Seattle, Washington, the
program recruits and trains community volunteers to protect the rights of severely
abused children, provide a one-on-one stable, adult relationship for an abused child,
and provide the court with an independent assessment to help the judge determine a
permanent placement for a child who will not be returning home.

CASA volunteers are appointed by the Juvenile Court to serve as advocates and
mentors for abused children going through dependency court proceedings. Unlike
social workers, therapists, and attorneys who juggle large caseloads and rarely
have time to focus on a single child, CASA volunteers work with only one child at a
time and often become the most important person in that child's life.

A CASA advocate visits with a child on a regular basis, interacts with all professionals involved in the case and makes recommendations directly to the court.

For other locations, visit the CASA website.

35

South Central Scholarship Fund

**South Central
Scholarship Fund**
Patricia London
1360 West 6th Street
305
San Pedro, CA 90732
trishahen@earthlink.net

Here is an opportunity to work with gifted, motivated students who want to go to college and become models and inspiration to other kids. Volunteers provide mentoring in the college preparation and application process, as well as in raising necessary scholarships and other funds.

The mission of the South Central Gifted Scholarship Fund is to aid, assist and partner with gifted, motivated high school students living in the South Central Los Angeles area who are attempting to transform their lives through education. The goal is to create a community of college graduates in South Central Los Angeles to serve as a resource to future students and to the fund as mentors, teachers and employers.

The Fund recognizes the cycle of poverty, despair and anguish that these young people have come through to reach the goal of "going to college." The organization helps these students become responsible adults who will come back to help their community and other students.

The Fund was founded in 2001, initially with the goal of assisting students with scholarships. These scholarships were meant to close the shortfalls between the amount of money offered in the financial packages from universities and the actual cost of a student's college education.

As the Board became familiar with the students and their college experiences, it became apparent that the students had needs above and beyond scholarship dollars. Most of the students lacked social, educational, and cultural experiences that would prepare them for success in college.

Even in the cases where the students have a family member or friend to encourage them, the person may not have any experience with college, college applications, financial aid packages and all of the necessary skills to assist the students. The Fund provides students with mentors and meaningful jobs to address these problems.

The Alliance for Children's Rights
Estelle Davis
(213) 368-6010 x127
kids-alliance.org

36

Getting Kids Adopted

Thousands of children are in foster homes and need adoptive parents. While retirees are typically too old to be appropriate parents, they can be active in motivating and assisting younger people to do it.

One of the organizations that are active in getting foster children placed with long-term parents is the Alliance for Children's Rights. It is Los Angeles County's only nonprofit free social services, legal help and information clearinghouse devoted solely to helping children living in poverty and foster care.

The Alliance's mission is to provide children the help and support they need to grow into healthy and productive adults. They currently help 6,000 children annually and have helped 30,000 since their founding in 1992.

They help children who need adoptive parents, are in the foster care system or about to leave foster care. With so many individuals and couples looking for children to adopt, there should be an opportunity to find good, permanent homes for these kids.

The Alliance can use your help. They are looking for volunteers who are willing to commit to at least eight hours a week, for a minimum of three months, to help carry out their mission.

37

Big Brothers Big Sisters

Big Brothers Big Sisters
230 North 13th Street
Philadelphia, PA 19107
(215) 567-7000
bbsa.org

Providing one-on-one mentoring to youth ages five to eighteen is the primary activity and mission of Big Brothers Big Sisters.

Founded in 1904, Big Brothers Big Sisters is the oldest and largest youth mentoring organization in the United States. In a typical past year, the organization served more than 200,000 youth in 5,000 communities across the Country, through a network of 470 agencies.

The BBBS one-on-one mentoring helps at-risk youth overcome the many challenges they face. Little Brothers and Sisters are less likely to begin using illegal drugs, consume alcohol, skip school and classes, or engage in acts of violence. They have greater self-esteem, confidence in their schoolwork performance, and are able to get along better with their friends and families.

Big Brothers Big Sisters was recently selected by Forbes Magazine as one of its top ten charities, making the publication's "gold star" list of charities which it believes are worthy of donor consideration, in its annual survey of 200 large charities.

'Big' volunteers provide 'Littles' with one-on-one time and attention in their schools, typically once a week during the academic year. Teachers identify children who can benefit most from interaction with a caring adult. As their friendships evolve, volunteers and children discover ways to make school and learning fun.

Stand Up For Kids
1510 Front Street,
 Suite 100
San Diego, CA
(800) 365-4543
standupforkids.org

38

Stand Up For Kids

The Stand Up For Kids mission is to help homeless and street kids. It is carried out by a national volunteer force of volunteers who try to find homeless kids and then work to improve their lives.

Since 1990, Stand Up For Kids has been walking the streets to rescue, educate, and involve homeless and at-risk youth. Their volunteers go to the streets to let troubled kids know that they have a friend that will listen—someone who will show them how to meet some of their immediate needs. Someone who will help provide them with the tools they need to get off the streets.

Through counseling, educational programs and skills training, their basic aim is to foster in these youth a sense of caring and self-confidence, give them access to information they need to lead productive lives, and help them realize their potential.

Most often, the street kids they see are alone and crying, dirty and hungry, misused and abused. They are struggling to survive and they believe that no one cares. Actually, for the most part, no one does. They are given hope by someone showing them that the past is not indicative of tomorrow.

Contact their website to find opportunities in your area.

**Foundation for
Teaching Economics**
260 Russell Blvd. Suite B
Davis, CA 95616
(530) 757-4630
fte.org

39

Foundation For
Teaching Economics

*Improving economic education is the basic mission of the
Foundation for Teaching Economics.*

For twenty-six years, the Foundation for Teaching Economics has had a commitment to quality in their programs to improve economic education. Throughout those years, the Board of Trustees has insisted that the Foundation engage only in undertakings of the highest merit in the teaching of economics.

Evaluation of the effectiveness of the FTE programs has led to major investments by the Gillette Company and the John Templeton Foundation. They share the FTE concern about economic education and value the FTE's reputation for quality and excellence.

The FTE web pages describe the current program offerings, along with other information. Enrollment in the FTE's new Economics Teachers Professional Association is burgeoning—with over 2,000 members.

There is no slackening in demand and, at the same time, the need to expose students to the lessons of market economics has never been greater.

America's Promise
909 North Washington
 Street, Suite 400
Alexandria, VA
22314-1556
(703) 684-4500
americaspromise.org

40

America's Promise

*An organization established to fulfill five basic commitments
to the Nation's children.*

America's Promise—The Alliance for Youth, led by General Colin Powell, is dedicated to mobilizing individuals, groups and organizations to build the character and competence of our youth.

At the heart of America's Promise is a set of five basic promises made to every child in America: an ongoing relationship with a caring adult—parent, mentor, tutor or coach; a safe place with structured activities during nonschool hours; a healthy start; a marketable skill through effective education; and an opportunity to give back through community services.

By working with America's Promise, you can support communities, strengthen the Nation and ensure a better future for our Nation's youth. There are several ways to join the America's Promise movement.

You can become part of a group of caring adults in more than 400 local Promise efforts across the Country, spending quality time with your young neighbors, looking them in the eye, believing in their potential, and inspiring them to achieve.

For other ways to help, visit their website.

41

Fulfillment Fund

Fulfillment Fund
1801 Avenue of the
Stars, Suite 250
Los Angeles, CA
90067
(310) 788-9700
fulfillment.org

The Fulfillment Fund's goal is to help economically disadvantaged students to graduate from high school and complete an advanced education.

The Fulfillment Fund is a nonprofit organization providing nearly 3,000 economically disadvantaged students with the resources, tools and skills needed to obtain quality educations and lead productive, fulfilling lives.

The program is one of total enrichment with one-on-one mentoring, classroom based outreach, college counseling, college scholarships, internships, career counseling and a parent education component.

Founded in 1977, the Fulfillment Fund's goal is to help students to graduate from high school and complete an advanced education. Comprehensive programs expose students to cultural and educational experiences that improve access to opportunities beyond their current reach.

You can help build a better tomorrow—one hour at a time. For more than twenty-five years they have been building their organization with the help of volunteers. They offer the satisfaction of knowing you are truly making a difference in the lives of deserving young scholars.

There are scores of activities from which to choose when you become a Fulfillment Fund volunteer.

MentorNet
c/o College of Engineering
San Jose State University
One Washington Square
San Jose, CA 95192-0080
(408) 924-4065
mentornet.net

42

MentorNet

MentorNet is an e-mentoring network that addresses the retention and success of women in engineering, science and mathematics.

Founded in 1997, MentorNet provides highly motivated protégés from many of the world's top colleges and universities with positive, one-on-one, email based mentoring relationships with mentors from industry and academia.

The MentorNet Community provides opportunities to connect with others from around the world who are interested in women's issues in engineering and science. Its primary goal is to provide mentoring to enhance persistence in fields where women remain underrepresented and to facilitate their entry into, and progression in, scientific and technical careers.

Other goals include extending its services to other groups: minority students, pre-college youth, young professionals, college and graduate students in other pre-professional fields in which women are underrepresented (e.g. economics, business), academic career mentors, entrepreneurs, and international participants and partners.

You can help by becoming an active MentorNet Community member, mentor or protégé, or by helping us to make your organization a MentorNet partner.

43

Halftime
2501 Cedar
Springs, Suite 200
Dallas, TX 75201
(214) 720-0878
halftime.org

Halftime

Halftime is focused on helping individuals get more out of life by making an effective transition from success to significance.

The Halftime organization presents an interactive, personalized coaching process for individuals looking to get more out of life, primarily with a faith-based bias. Their view is that 'Halftime' is a journey—a process of transitioning from success to significance that can happen over months or even years.

Halftime provides ideas, stories and self-assessment tools to assist people in their transition. The program is built around these beliefs and attitudes:

"Halftime is a pause in the middle of the game of life to reflect on who we are and what really matters to us and to redirect our time and resources for the second half. It is a time when the quest for success loses meaning, and we ask, 'Is this it? I've achieved some level of accomplishment, and done much of what I set out to do. What's next?' We want our lives to have really counted for something, something that will live on long after we are gone. We want to move beyond success to significance. Most call this a midlife crisis. We call it halftime."

When you create an online profile, you will begin receiving 'My Halftime Guide' which includes resources, suggestions, real life stories, and information that is fine-tuned to your phase of life. You will also have access to event schedules and The Halftime Report, a monthly newsletter featuring individuals who have found significance in their second halves.

Understanding which phase of Halftime you are currently traveling through will help you find the resources you need to keep moving forward, such as ideas, tips, assessment tools, stories, and books. Their Leadership Network is a program that puts on five-day training institutes for volunteer resources directors in churches.

Religious, Faith Based, Spiritual

A recent Gallup poll found that eighty-four percent of Americans long for spirituality. Many medical studies have linked the benefits of a spiritual practice to improved mental health.

There are many kinds of spirituality. A general definition is 'a search for meaning and mission in life.' Humans tend to be predisposed to want to embrace a higher power. As they age, individuals increasingly regard religion as an important way to define, or redefine who they are. Others may seek non-religious ways of being spiritual.

Individuals who are interested in becoming active in religious or faith based programs can probably best get started at their own church. If you are not active in a local church, there are many who would welcome your involvement.

Some of the larger religious organizations that will welcome your involvement are mentioned here. These organizations can also be helpful if you want to initiate some type of special religious activity in your own community.

A more general concept of spirituality might be the focus on one's 'inner life.' This is contrasted to a person's 'outer life'—career, family, home, physical possessions. We have identified programs that relate more to the general search for spirituality.

The following suggestions can help you locate activities and organizations that can get you started on your spiritual quest.

Christianity Today
465 Gundersen Drive
Carol Stream, IL 60188
(630) 260-6200
ChristianityToday.com

44

Christianity Today
Magazine

Christianity Today is a leading publication about religious activities and is a source of contacts for individuals looking for opportunities to get more active in Christian programs.

Christianity Today's founder and honorary chairman is Billy Graham. Its website is an excellent place to start a general exploration of opportunities to become active in religious activities, especially if you don't have a current church or religious affiliation.

The online publication has a classified ad section for individuals seeking positions, and chat and message board areas on topics such as women, men, marriage, parenting, singles, teens, and kids.

The International area allows for connections to multi-language Christian sites and resources around the world, as well as Christianity Today International's own coverage of global issues and events. It has a translator to read the articles in other languages.

In the Bible Studies area you can find Christian fellowship and spiritual encouragement from people who share the same interests.

The Message Boards have hundreds of discussions covering today's hot topics, denominations, spiritual life, prayer, family concerns, and others.

**Park Cities
Presbyterian
Church**
4124 Oak Lawn
  Avenue
Dallas, TX 75219
(214) 224-2500
pcpc.org

45

Park Cities Presbyterian Church

This is one of the many large churches that provide resources for churches and opportunities for individuals nationwide.

Park Cities Presbyterian Church, located in Dallas Texas, presents placement opportunities for those interested in serving a church. It has developed more than 2,500 placement opportunities over its history.

The Park Cities congregation is a member of the Presbyterian Church in America (PCA). The PCA was founded in 1973 in response to the need for a scriptural, evangelical and reformed witness to Christ. It has established as its top priorities to be biblical in both its government and doctrine and committed to evangelism, Christian education, and the equipping of Christians for ministry.

The Mission to North America at PCPC has started churches in Austin, McKinney, and Houston, Texas and is partnering with the Southwest Church Planting Network in beginning other new churches and establishing new campus ministries.

PCPC's World Missions Ministry has as its purpose the extension of its presence to people in locations outside the borders of the United States. It has as its vision the planting of 100 churches in various countries by the year 2020.

46

Renew International

Renew
International
1232 George Street
Plainfield, NJ 07062
(908) 769-5400
renewintl.org

Renew is a program developed within the Catholic church, but applicable to other Christian organizations to bring together small groups to focus on spiritual renewal.

Renew International, a Roman Catholic organization, fosters spiritual renewal, evangelization and the transformation of the world through parish-based small Christian communities.

Their parish renewal process and small Christian community materials offer spiritual information and motivation to help people courageously live out their faith and give witness to Jesus Christ. Their services offer thorough training, sound materials and a network of pastoral support.

Renew reaches out to young adults and families; is involved on college and university campuses; works simultaneously with English and Spanish speaking peoples; conducts trainings; offers pastoral consultation; and publishes resources for the Renew process. Renew has a special outreach to the hearing impaired, sight impaired, African-American community and prison ministry.

Renew Worldwide is Renew International's outreach to countries beyond North America. The Spirit of God has led them to minister to people on every inhabited continent, sharing the incredibly Good News of Jesus Christ.

Small Christian communities are the key strategy for implementing the new evangelization. A special Small Christian Community (SCC) Team is available to work with parishes and dioceses for the ongoing development and growth of parish-based small communities.

Saddleback Valley Community Church
One Saddleback
 Parkway
Lake Forest, CA
 92630
(949) 609-8000
saddleback.com

47

Saddleback Church

Saddleback Church's pastor is the creator of the book that has provided inspiration for millions to reassess their lives and to find meaningful purpose.

More than 200,000 church leaders from around the world have been trained in Saddleback's purpose-driven philosophy.

Saddleback's pastor Rick Warren's book, *The Purpose Driven Life*, has been on the New York Times bestseller list for forty-five weeks and has sold over eleven million copies. It focuses on the message that life is "not about you," and shows how God can enable each of us to live for His purposes.

When Rick and Kay Warren first arrived in the Saddleback Valley in January 1980, all they had was what they could fit in the back of a U-Haul truck. Fresh out of seminary, and with many good Bible-teaching churches already in Southern California, Pastor Rick turned his attention to those who didn't attend church regularly.

They began with a small Bible study, meeting with one other family in the Warrens' small condo. On Easter of 1980, Saddleback Valley Community Church held its very first public service and 205 people, most of whom had never been to church, showed up.

Saddleback Church now has more than 200 ministries serving the church and community. More and more believers over fifty years of age are exchanging their 'career' for a 'mission', getting involved with missions around the world. From two-year stints on, these 'Masters' are bringing a whole new wealth into the missionary movement.

48

Willow Creek Association

Willow Creek Association
Willow Creek Community Church
P.O. Box 3188
Barrington, IL 60011-3188
(847) 765-0070
willowcreek.org

The Willow Creek Association is a center for churches nationwide interested in developing strategic programs and training church leaders.

Since 1992, the Willow Creek Association, an activity of the Willow Creek Community Church of Barrington Illinois, has been linking like-minded, action-oriented churches with each other and with strategic vision, training, and resources.

The WCA works to equip Member Churches and others with the tools needed to build prevailing churches everywhere in the world.

Their primary desire is to inspire, equip, and encourage Christian leaders to build biblically functioning churches that reach increasing numbers of unchurched people—not just with innovations from the Willow Creek Association or Willow Creek Community Church, but with God-given breakthroughs with widespread potential from any church in the world.

A key component of this God-honoring movement is to provide strategic vision and practical training.

More than 9,500 churches around the world are a part of the Willow Creek Association. In 2003 alone, more than 100,000 local church leaders, staff, and volunteers—from Member Churches and others—attended one of their conferences or training events.

A Course in Miracles

Foundation for
Inner Peace
PO Box 598
Mill Valley, CA
94942-0598
acim.org

49

A Course In Miracles

*A basic course for those seeking to strengthen their spiritual beliefs
and the importance of love in their relationships.*

A Course in Miracles is a complete self-study spiritual thought system, a three-volume curriculum consisting of a Text, Workbook for Students, and Manual for Teachers. The Course focuses on the healing of relationships and making them holy. Even though the language of the Course is that of traditional Christianity, it expresses a non-sectarian, non-denominational spirituality. *A Course in Miracles* is a universal spiritual teaching, not a religion.

The "Workbook for Students" consists of 365 lessons, an exercise for each day of the year. This one-year training program begins the process of changing the student's mind and perception, though it is not intended to bring one's learning to completion. *A Course in Miracles* was first published in 1975, the year the founder, Dr. Schucman assigned copyright of the Course to the Foundation for Inner Peace (FIP). Since the beginning and as designated, this Foundation has been its publisher, disseminator, and copyright/trademark holder, although in 1999 it assigned the copyright and trademark to the Foundation for A Course in Miracles (FACIM). There are currently over one and a half million copies of the Course in circulation worldwide.

The summary introduction, which appears in its Text, is quite succinct and brief. It reads: "This is a course in miracles. It is a required course. Only the time you take it is voluntary. Free will does not mean that you can establish the curriculum. It means only that you can elect what you want to take at a given time. The course does not aim at teaching the meaning of love, for that is beyond what can be taught. It does aim, however, at removing the blocks to the awareness of love's presence, which is your natural inheritance. The opposite of love is fear, but what is all-encompassing can have no opposite."

50

Christian Employment Resource

Christian Employment Resource
1525 Aviation Blvd.,
Suite 428
Redondo Beach, CA
90278
(310) 374-0701
christianemployment.org

A website developed to provide employment assistance to churches and other religious based organizations, and to individuals seeking opportunities.

In 1998 Christian Employment Resource (on-line) was started to utilize the Internet as a tool to communicate with Christian job seekers worldwide. 1999 marked the year of expanding the ministry to the world with an outreach to other churches and ministries worldwide addressing their specific employment needs.

Christian Employment Resource now has a subscriber list of over 16,000 churches, ministries, job-seekers and Christian businesses. It is a non-denominational organization with no direct association or affiliation with any Christian organization. The principles are solidly rooted in biblical principles.

The main focus is to raise the standard to those in the body of Christ and educate them on how Christ works in their job/career life as well. Not just on Sundays. The mission from the outset was to equip clients with 'real world' methods on how the job search works and not from hearsay.

They believe in providing a biblical based approach to unemployment and career transitions. While anchored in the Word, they also teach cutting-edge, non-orthodox methods enabling Christians to understand the many methods that are time-wasters and contribute to frustration and depression.

Would you like to start a Christian Employment Support Group at your church? Just email CER at job@christianemployment.com with your name and email address saying "Send me support group materials" and they will send you the details.

If you are looking for employment, see their website.

51

Alternative Spiritual Paths

*Information for those seeking spiritual inspiration and opportunity
beyond the more traditional religious programs.*

Body & Soul magazine recently ran an article on this subject, "How Spirit Blooms" (September 2004). In addition to discussing ways of getting closer to God, they also touched on other spiritual practices. These include:

Buddhism—the fourth largest religion in the world, with roots in India, 525 B.C., where Prince Siddhartha received enlightenment under the bodhi tree at the river Neranjara. Thereafter, he was known as the Buddha, or Awakened One. Buddhism is based on the theory that life is a continual cycle of birth, death and rebirth, and that we live in constant suffering. Meditation, persistent self-inquiry, and observance of moral precepts are the way to Liberation and freedom from suffering. Sects include Theravada, Tibetan, Mahayana, and Zen.

Yoga—which means "union" in sanskrit, has its roots in India in the 4th century B.C. It is a practice of unifying with the divine Self, the Self that exists beyond the ego, or small self. Yogis maintain that through physical, psychological and spiritual practice we can transcend the small ego-driven chatter of our minds.

Sufism—first brought to America by Hazrat Inayat Khan in 1910. It is best known as the mystical movement within the Islamic religion, emphasizing personal union with the divine.

Wicca—is derived from pre-Christian Celtic religion. An earth based religion, with an emphasis on preserving nature and working with natural forces to create harmony and healing. They believe in a ubiquitous force, which they refer to as the All or the One, and are guided by the cycles of nature, symbols, and deities of ancient Celtic society.

52

Spiritual Eldering Institute

Spiritual Eldering Institute
7318 Germantown Avenue
Philadelphia, PA 19919
(888) ELD-RING
spiritualeldering.org

An organization assisting seniors in reviewing their lives and developing legacies for future generations.

The Spiritual Eldering Institute is a multi-faith organization dedicated to the spiritual dimensions of aging and conscious living and to affirming the importance of the elder years.

The Institute provides workshops nationwide that guide elders in reviewing their lives, harvesting the wisdom of their years, and transmitting a legacy to future generations.

It encourages the formation of local spiritual eldering groups, and provides a leaders training program for those interested in becoming facilitators.

In spiritual eldering, we talk about the many organisms which we inhabit: the physical being, the energy body, our organism of affect, all the people we care for, our organism of mind which inhabits all our intellectual worlds, and, ultimately, our spirit.

Challenge your thinking and assumptions. Sign up to grow. Exercise your imagination. Find your source in contemplative practice. Join friends. Share your story. Find a place of service. Give yourself permission to live your best life. Discover your gifts.

University of Creation Spirituality
Naropa University
 Oakland Campus
2141 Broadway
Oakland, CA
 94612-2309
(510) 835-4827
creationspirituality.com

53

Creation Spirituality

A program for individuals to work at finding their true self by integrating western spirituality with scientific understanding of the universe.

Creation Spirituality honors all of creation as an original blessing. Creation Spirituality integrates the wisdom of western spirituality and global indigenous cultures with the emerging post-modern scientific understanding of the universe and the awakening artistic passion for creativity which reveals the interrelatedness of all beings.

The Creation Spirituality movement seeks to integrate the wisdom of western spirituality and global indigenous cultures with the emerging scientific understanding of the universe and the passionate creativity of art.

Creation Spirituality believes that the universe is basically a blessing, that is, something we experience as good; we can and do relate to the universe as a whole since we are a microcosm of that macrocosm and that this relationship "intoxicates" us (Aquinas); everyone is a mystic (i.e., born full of wonder and capable of recovering it at any age; of not taking the awe and wonder of existence for granted); everyone is a prophet, i.e., a "mystic in action" (Hocking) who is called to "interfere" (Heschel) with what interrupts authentic life.

They believe that humans have to dig and work at finding their deep self, their true self, their spirit self; thus the role of spiritual praxis and meditation and community confrontation which can itself be a yoga. If we do not undergo such praxis we live superficially out of fear or greed or addiction or someone else's expectations of us. That salvation is best understood as "preserving the good" (Aquinas).

54

Spirituality.com

*An Internet community for those looking for understanding of spirituality
in order to make a difference in the world.*

Millions of spiritual seekers are finding that spirituality is bigger than any one category or definition. And they are finding connections with spirituality throughout their life experiences—it's a substantial part of their identity and is a goodness that is universal, impartial and available to meet any need.

Spirituality.com is a Web community for anyone seeking a deeper understanding of spirituality and life in order to make a difference in the world. It is a resource for every individual's spiritual journey.

The book *Science and Health with Key to the Scriptures* by Mary Baker Eddy is the inspiration for this site—it is a premier spirituality sourcebook and was written for every seeker to read and explore. In writing and publishing *Science and Health*, Eddy wanted to make the healing system she discovered through her own spiritual journey available to the whole world. That is why she dedicates her book to all "honest seekers for Truth."

The site provides a meeting place for you to interact with a growing community of seekers and to benefit from the spiritual insights found in Eddy's book, in community-generated articles and in the community dialogues. Open discussion areas, a 24/7 chat and live Q&A events featuring spiritual thought leaders and fellow spiritual travelers are also available for you to participate in or read.

Employment

*M*any individuals who are completing their tour of full-time employment look forward to their leisure and discretionary time and to helping others on a volunteer basis. Others may have reasons to explore alternative employment opportunities.

These individuals may decide they need or want additional income, or they may decide that they can only get recognition and personal satisfaction if they are being paid for their abilities and efforts.

AARP reports that eighty percent of baby boomers plan to work during their retirement years. A recent survey reported in the Journal of Financial Planning of pre-retirees and working retirees between the ages of fifty and seventy showed that forty-five percent expect to work into their seventies, and eighteen percent into their eighties, either out of desire, financial necessity, or both. The survey found that fifty-four percent cited the need for money and sixty-six percent listed health benefits as primary motivating factors.

The desire to stay mentally active (eighty-seven percent), physically active (eighty-five percent), and productive or useful (seventy-seven percent) were other primary motivating factors. Twenty-seven percent expect to work in a different field.

The following pages provide some suggestions and ways of exploring alternative employment opportunities, full or part time. We have not included any 'working at home' suggestions.

Monster.com
HotJobs.com
Careerbuilder.com
Headhunter.net

55

Job Hunting
on the Internet

*There are many job search sites on the Internet. Using them is
easy and typically free or low cost.*

The reality is that the older you are, the more difficult it is to find a new job using traditional approaches. It is much better to use your special insights, experience and contacts to find that position for which you may be uniquely, or at least specially suited.

If you do need to open up your scope of search, the Internet can be very helpful. There are the big job sites that provide helpful advice and articles, as well as resume and cover letter suggestions and examples. You can scan their job listings and then email the contact person directly. Some of the leading sites are shown above.

A variation on this approach is to use those sites for learning about an interesting job opening, and then use your own networking contacts to learn who you should be talking to in that company about that specific situation. Applying directly through the website will take you directly to the human resources department, where you may or may not collect your $200.

If you have specialized professional skills and experience, you can look for niche sites related to your field of interest. Many of these specialized trade or industry sites have job listings and other career help. Some allow you to post your resume confidentially.

Posting your resume online is generally frowned upon by the experts. Only about four to six percent of job seekers find jobs this way, and the sites are not at all private. A representative of the Privacy Foundation stated that resumes might be stored by online job sites for many years and may be misused for data mining and identity theft.

linkedin.com
Openbc.com
Zerodegrees.com
Tribe.net
Careerchangenetwork.com
Alwaysonnetwork.com
Ecademy.com
Friendster.com
ExecuNet.com

56

Social Networking

Retirees looking for employment should consider using the several online 'social networks' in their job seeking efforts.

Unlike regular employment sites, which mainly list want ads and applicants' resumes, social networks are designed to allow individuals to interact socially.

When job seeking, the idea isn't necessarily to search for a specific opening. Instead, you look for other members who have a common friend or interest. From there you build a relationship by email and meetings, just as you would in traditional networking.

Fans of the networks claim that the personal connection with other members gets them access to choice jobs that don't show up in want ads. The networks can put individuals in touch with top executives instead of just the human-resource officials they would reach through an ad.

Professionally oriented social networks have existed for years, but only in the past few months have the social networks bloomed, due largely to the success of Friendster.com, a network that lets you meet new people through others whom you know in common.

These networks are not limited to job seeking; they are used for many business purposes, including just getting to know others in companies in which you may have an interest. Providers and users warn that on average, it can take months to realize an online network's full benefits, so don't expect overnight results.

There are several services that have recently come online. Because they are relatively new, and they are trying to build their markets, many of the services are currently free of charge to the job seeker. However, that could change as they become more successful. Here are several to consider.

57

Career One Stop

Career One Stop
careeronestop.org
America's Job Bank
ajb.org
America's CareerInfonet
acinet.org
America's Service Locator
servicelocator.org

Career One Stop is an Internet based job search service funded by the U.S. Department of Labor.

Career One Stop is a gateway to job listings (both full-time and part-time), resumes, and career information nationwide. It comprises three main services that work together to offer solutions to the demands of today's labor market. There are no fees to use any of their services.

America's Job Bank is the biggest and busiest job market in cyberspace. Job seekers can post their resume where thousands of employers search every day, search for job openings automatically, and find their dream job fast.

America's CareerInfonet is your information source for smart career decisions. Users can find wage and employment trends, occupational requirements, state-by-state labor markets and resources, millions of employer contacts, handy career tools and more.

America's Service Locator (and toll-free Help Line) work together to provide a comprehensive database of service providers accessible to the public via the Internet or phone. America's Service Locator directs customers to a range of services available in their area, including education opportunities, disabled or older worker programs and much more.

58

Senior Job Bank

Senior Job Bank exists to spread the word about the wisdom of keeping our older population in the workforce longer.

With this website, Eric Summers revived a service he began in 1975 through newspaper ads in Florida. The Senior Job Bank website offers an easy, effective and free method for senior citizens to find occasional, part-time, flexible, temporary and even full-time jobs.

Through the Senior Job Bank website, homeowners and businesses deal directly with older, more mature, more experienced and more reliable workers.

The Senior Job Bank encourages government, nonprofit organizations and businesses to work together to solve problems in our society. They provide links to business, government and nonprofit services relative to jobs for our senior citizens.

It encourages government, nonprofit organizations and businesses to work together to help seniors find 'meaningful' jobs. Senior Job Bank provides free links to sites that are relative to jobs for older workers.

Senior Job Bank attracted national news in 1980 because of their refusal to accept Federal grants. They enjoyed the support of many nationally known politicians, including Congressman Claude Pepper, Sen. Lawton Chiles and Howard Jarvis (Proposition 13), as well as CEO's of major national corporations and nonprofit organizations.

59

Experience Works

Experience Works, Inc
2200 Clarendon Blvd,
Suite 1000
Arlington, VA 22201
(866) 397-9757
experienceworks.org

Experience Works is a national, nonprofit organization that provides training and employment services for mature workers.

Established in 1965 as Green Thumb, and renamed Experience Works in 2002, the organization reaches more than 125,000 mature individuals in all fifty states and Puerto Rico each year.

Experience Works has more than 400 employees, offices in thirty-eight states and Puerto Rico, and is the largest grantee of the Federal government's Senior Community Service Employment Program (SCSEP).

In 1995, Experience Works started the first nationwide staffing service specifically designed for mature workers regardless of their age and income. SCSEP efforts benefited nearly 29,000 seniors last program year, is provided funding by more than seventy public and private sources, and operates on a total budget of more than $100 million.

Experience Works operates older-worker training projects across the Country. These projects involve occupational skills, on-the-job training, and classroom training.

The participating employer receives partial reimbursement for the extraordinary costs that may be associated with training the particular individual.

**International
Rescue Committee**
122 East 42nd Street
New York, NY 10168
(212) 551-3000
theirc.org

60

International
Rescue Committee

*The International Rescue Committee helps people fleeing racial, religious
and ethnic persecution, as well as those uprooted by war and violence.*

Founded in 1933, the International Rescue Committee is a world leader in relief, rehabilitation, protection, post-conflict development, resettlement services and advocacy for those uprooted or affected by violent conflict and oppression.

At work in twenty-five countries, the IRC delivers lifesaving aid in emergencies, rebuilds shattered communities, cares for war-traumatized children, rehabilitates health care, water and sanitation systems, reunites separated families, restores lost livelihoods, establishes schools, trains teachers, strengthens the capacity of local organizations and supports civil society and good-governance initiatives.

The IRC helps thousands of refugees resettle in the United States every year, and their offices across the Country make sure that all new arrivals receive shelter, food and clothing. They also provide recently arrived refugees with translation services, English-language instruction, job training, employment services and other counseling. They are vocal public policy advocates, calling attention to critical issues affecting refugees around the world.

The IRC looks for people with strong cross-cultural social skills who are also good community organizers. The ability to adapt and work as a team player is important. Much of the work takes place in emergency situations, so the ability to work under pressure and in unstable security environments is often required.

They look for: a commitment to their mission and the job; a desire to help; requisite technical background and skills for the job; willingness to be a team player; and a professional manner that reflects respect, trust, self-confidence, flexibility, perseverance, and diplomacy.

FilmAid International
215 West 125th Street,
Suite 3F
New York, NY 10027
(646) 284-9696
filmaidinternational.org

61

Executive Director For Not-For-Profits

Many charitable and other not-for-profits are looking for experienced business executives to serve as the administrative and fundraising leaders of their organizations.

Nonprofit organizations are typically looking for individuals with management skills and the ability to reach out into the business and professional communities for fund raising.

These positions can be rewarding in terms of learning about the specific activities of the group, meeting new and interesting friends, and the opportunity to keep your business contacts alive.

An example of a recent need was FilmAid International, a humanitarian aid organization founded in 1999, which shows films to refugees. The films, mostly dramas meant to entertain and inspire, as well as educate about public health, often attract 15,000 refugees or more.

The group first offered films in Kosovo and now operates in Kenya and Tanzania. It is headquartered in New York City.

There are hundreds of groups looking for leadership. Many of the leading executive search firms can help put you into contact with organizations in your area.

If you can't find a not-for-profit that appeals to you, create one to meet a need that you have identified.

New Directions
66 Long Wharf
Boston, MA
02110-3620
(617) 523-7775
newdirections.com

62

New Directions

*New Directions works exclusively with leaders in the corporate,
professional and public arenas, guiding them through work
and life transitions to new opportunities.*

For seventeen years, New Directions' work has centered on helping clients find new full-time positions. They also help launch clients into entrepreneurial ventures, consulting practices and new careers.

New Directions provides all clients the opportunity to first explore and, if interested, immerse themselves in expertly designed programs focused on entrepreneurial ventures, consulting businesses, board directorships, nonprofit endeavors, or public service.

For baby boomers seeking alternatives to passive retirement—now or within a few years—New Directions' nationally recognized Life Portfolio Program helps them develop a balance of part-time work with other meaningful activities.

These might include family and leisure time, continued learning, teaching or "giving back"—as many of their clients already do through their Foundation for New Directions.

63

Boardseat

*BoardSeat is a resource for those looking for seats on boards
of directors or advisory board positions.*

The firm is based in San Francisco and is the leading independent executive search company focusing exclusively on director and advisory board searches and consulting.

Founded by Stephen Fowler, a former Silicon Valley venture capitalist who recognized the need of many companies for stronger boards and advisory boards, BoardSeat's services are designed to meet these needs. Their primary focus is on public and venture-backed companies.

BoardSeat carries out placements for board directors and advisory board members. They have recently completed the first ever survey into the compensation and administration of boards of directors and advisory boards of venture-backed companies.

BoardSeat offers free and confidential entry onto their database of potential board members. They encourage membership from executives, professionals, academics and others whose experience, skills and contacts are likely to be of interest to their clients.

The benefits of membership in BoardSeat include free lifetime membership; consideration for director positions; and consideration for advisory board positions.

ConsultingBase Ltd
c/o EME
3 Millharbour
London, E14 9XP
+44 (0)20 7987 3294
consultingbase.com

64

Consulting Base

*A networking and information service for those interested
in consulting in emerging markets.*

Consulting Base is an information and contact exchange for consulting opportunities in emerging markets and developing countries. It serves professional advisors and firms and provides expertise, knowledge and procurement information.

On their site you can register as a consultant, register your firm, search consulting job ads and search projects.

Their Country Information Section provides a combination of analysis, current news and travel tools from a range of emerging markets and developing countries.

Up-to-date country briefings provide an overview of the history and demography for 193 countries, including analyses of the key sectors within those countries.

Consulting Base provides a wide range of other online services for international development consultants, consulting firms and other organizations in the industry.

65

Directors Register

*The Directors Register provides match-making services to companies
and individuals related to service on boards of directors.*

The Register provides an opportunity for individuals with board level abilities to showcase their interest and willingness to serve on a board of directors. It also provides a facility for companies looking to identify qualified, talented, experienced individuals interested and willing to serve as a member of their board of directors.

Attracting the "right" outside directors is critically important to both mature companies and those start-ups looking to raise capital. For the public, or soon to be public company, the quality of outside directors says volumes about management and the prospects of the company.

First class directors are hard to attract and tend to serve on those company boards that have talented management and excellent products and services. Shareholders look to the outside board members as their representatives at the company and may form opinions of the quality of the company based on the pedigree and experience of the outside board.

Young companies need competent, experienced outside board members for the very same reasons. At the capital raising stage of these companies, outside board members provide credibility that the young entrepreneur needs to help convince investors that their company has a bright future.

Entrepreneuring, New Ventures, Business

*F*or those who have a business background, or those who always wanted to start a business but didn't have the opportunity, starting or acquiring a business might be attractive.

However, as we cautioned earlier, a person who is retired, or considering retirement should be careful about getting over-committed to something that can be quite expensive and time-consuming. Continuity in a business venture can be critical. You don't want to have to bail out at the wrong time.

On the other hand, if you have a son or daughter, or some other younger person you are close to who might want to take on a new venture, the helping process can be quite rewarding in terms of the activity and satisfaction, and also potentially profitable.

If you are considering the entrepreneurial route, you might benefit from some words of wisdom from the *Wall Street Journal*'s Startup.com website: "Funding mistakes can be fatal; entrepreneurs are proverbial optimists, not seeing the difficulties in generating sales and underestimating expenses. So one of the classic errors is not having or raising enough capital."

A related problem is the failure to keep accurate and timely financial records. When tax time comes around, it's nearly impossible to reconstruct income and expenses. The idea of paying taxes in advance is often a surprise to owners who were previously employees. The quarterly tax bill includes not only estimated income taxes, but also such self-employment taxes as Social Security and Medicare.

For a small start-up, coming up with $1,000 to $2,000 every three months for Uncle Sam can be painful. You may remember you need to make payroll, but you forget about the extra $3,000 you need at tax time, so you rob from Peter to pay Paul, and that's when you run into trouble,

In addition to some general business and investment ideas, we have presented a few franchise offerings, just as a sample of the broad range of what might be available. We are not endorsing or recommending any of them; you must be sure to do your homework on any franchise proposal.

66

Startup Journal

StartupJournal is a Wall Street Journal website for entrepreneurs.

Starting your own business or buying a franchise is tough, even in a strong economy. You'll have to research the market, secure financing, open a shop, hire employees and run the enterprise.

StartupJournal can help. Their content comes from the powerful editorial resources of *The Wall Street Journal*, the world's leading business publication, as well as WSJ.com, industry experts and StartupJournal's editorial team.

When you visit startupjournal.com, you'll see their main page, which lists current stories and leads to the WSJ extensive resources. The main page is updated every business day, so you can visit it often to keep up on the news and trends that affect you.

Browse online databases of thousands of existing companies from around the Country and abroad that are for sale.

Are you looking to purchase a franchise? From retailing to professional services, find the franchising opportunity that's right for you.

BizBuySell.com. Inc.
1110 Burlingame
 Avenue, Suite 202
Burlingame, CA 94010
(650) 373-2900
bizbuysell.com

67

BizBuySell

*For finding a business to buy, or to sell, or to find a business broker, bizbuysell.com
is hard to beat. It can also be a lead to becoming a business broker.*

BizBuySell.com is the largest and most heavily trafficked online exchange for businesses for sale, with more business for sale listings, more users, and more search activity than any other service.

BizBuySell has an inventory of over 27,000 businesses for sale, and more than 400,000 visitors search the site each month. BizBuySell also has one of the largest databases of sale comparables for recently sold businesses.

The company was founded in 1996. The BizBuySell marketplace consists of not only established businesses for sale, but also asset sales, franchise opportunities and business real estate.

It also can put you in contact with business brokers working in your area. BizBuySell currently has over 1,700 business brokers subscribing to BizBuySell's BrokerWorks service. Broker members can list multiple businesses for sale and can contact registered buyers.

Broker members are provided with a web page to promote their business on the Internet, and are included in BrokerPages, the premier directory of business brokers on the Internet.

Sparkplug
sparkplug.com
**Cabot Advisory
Group**
cabotgrp.com

68

Create A Virtual Company

*One way to enjoy the challenge and benefits of starting your own
company, without many of the negative aspects of being an entrepreneur,
is to create a 'virtual' business.*

A virtual company has no central office, minimal overhead, and can even go into hibernation if circumstances require it. Many people who have started and/or worked for virtual businesses cannot imagine working in a regular office again.

In a true virtual company, contact among co-workers is maintained via the Internet on high-speed connections and through email and telephone calls. Co-workers may meet with one another at the beginning of a new project. Periodic face-to-face meetings with team members or clients can be held at any one of a number of 'branch' offices; typically the nearest Starbucks or McDonalds.

If more prestigious accommodations are required for client meetings, the many executive suite operations can provide meeting rooms on a pay-as-you-use basis.

An example of a virtual company is Sparkplug, a design firm founded in 1997. The founding partners moved from the San Francisco area to the much lower cost living in Olympia, Washington. They now have seven main employees, spread from Vancouver, Washington to Laguna Niguel in Southern California, plus seven others who are called on as needed. With their extremely low overhead many of the employees are able to enjoy six-figure incomes. And, with fixed expenses essentially non-existent, the firm can ride out slow business periods readily without going into the red.

Another example is Cabot Advisory Group, made up of individuals who formerly worked as human resource directors at major corporations such as GTE, Texas Instruments, Xerox and Hewlett-Packard. They advise clients on how to best handle the people aspect of mergers or acquisitions.

National Association of
Seed and Venture Funds
nasvf.org
**Southern California
Investment Association**
sciaonline.org
**Tech Coast Venture
Network**
tcvn.org
Tech Coast Angels
Irvine, CA
techcoastangels.com

69

New Venture Investment

Join or start an investment group to help new ventures get started and prosper.

There are many small investment groups that have been formed, particularly in the locations where the larger venture capital firms are located. Individuals living in those areas can find "angel" investment groups to join. Those living in areas with no such groups can help start one.

A typical angel group will meet to discuss new company investment opportunities and evaluate business plans. Those who are intrigued with an opportunity will help fund it and serve on the new company board, or become part-time management in its early stages.

These groups are particularly well suited to individuals with strong business backgrounds and operating experience. Typically, participants are expected to commit to a certain level of annual investment, but each decision is left to the individual. $50,000 per year is typical.

The National Association of Seed and Venture Funds is an organization of private, public and nonprofit organizations committed to building their local economies by investing and facilitating investment in local entrepreneurs.

Above are other contacts for those wanting more information on investing and becoming active in these new ventures.

70

Follow VC
Investment Activities

While it can be fun and potentially profitable, new venture investing can also be a good way to lose a lot of money. Keeping track of new venture investment by the pros is helpful in minimizing mistakes.

There are many investment firms that have billions of dollars to invest in a wide array of new business ideas. It is not the best arena for the smaller investor with limited capital. Particularly if they cannot afford to lose that capital.

A way to keep track of and to capitalize on what the big investor groups are funding, is to subscribe to a service that keeps track of what the venture-backed new firms are doing, the start-up management teams and the professionals that do business with them.

The Dow Jones VentureWire Professional is one of the services available that track new venture investment. It provides daily coverage of the latest VC news, current deals, future financing plans and forward market trends. They keep you informed of key executive moves, board level changes and new partners.

The service allows you to search over 40,000 venture financings, M & A's and other news. This information can help you anticipate upcoming IPO's, and to be aware of new technologies or applications that can help you anticipate implications for the more established companies.

It may also help you spot consulting or board opportunities with companies in fields in which you may have expertise. The service is not inexpensive, but can be worthwhile for those who can benefit, either financially or vicariously.

71

Find Grant Opportunities

Applying for grants to get your research or new business off the ground is one way to find needed capital.

If you have an idea in any field, you may want to explore the possibility of obtaining grant support to fund the early research and development of the idea.

The charter of grants.gov is to provide a simple, unified electronic storefront for interactions between grant applicants and the Federal agencies that manage grant funds. There are twenty-six Federal grant-making agencies and over 900 individual grant programs that award over $350 billion in grants each year.

The grant community includes state, local and tribal governments, academia and research institutions, and not-for-profits.

Obtaining grants is not easy; many individuals and organizations are competing for a limited supply of funds. However, the effort itself can open many doors and allow you to meet many interesting and talented people.

Typically, you need to associate with an existing organization that has established itself as a research group, or an institution with special credentials in your general field of interest. Through one or more of those organizations you can begin searching for grant opportunities.

Grants.gov provides organizations with the ability to search for Federal government-wide grant opportunities. There are leads to over thirty government agencies that are interested in providing grants in areas of interest to their areas of specialization.

The Office of Federal Financial Management recently issued a policy directive requiring that all agencies post grant opportunities online as of November 7, 2004. To begin your search for grant opportunities, access Search Grant Opportunities on the website.

You can register to receive all email notifications of new grant postings by going to Receive Grant Opportunity Notification on the site.

72

Social Entrepreneuring

Chesapeake Habitat for Humanity
chesapeakehfh.org/teambuilds
Net Impact
netimpact.org
AccessWorld Solutions (American Foundation for the Blind)
afb.org/aw

Bringing for-profit entrepreneurial ideas and skills to nonprofit organizations that are working to improve society can have profound positive impact.

Many not-for-profit organizations are adopting for-profit activities to help support their core programs. Using the skills and market knowledge developed through their nonprofit activities, many organizations are learning to raise additional funds for their core mission. This is helping them to be more effective both in what they do and how they raise the money to do it.

The Goldman Sachs Foundation Partnership on Nonprofit Ventures sponsors an annual competition in which nonprofits submit for-profit venture ideas and compete for prize money and consulting services.

The Habitat for Humanity organization in the Baltimore area has launched a for-profit venture called TeamBuilds, where corporate teams pay $7,500 for an all-day team-building session while they work together to rebuild an old house. They believe they can raise about $100,000 for the organization during its first full year in operation.

Organizations such as Net Impact are connecting people interested in this 'social entrepreneurship' concept. It has become an acceptable, teachable concept, now being taught in a number of leading business schools throughout the Country.

AccessWorld Solutions was started in 2002 by the American Foundation for the Blind to help major corporations such as Adobe Systems and Cisco Systems make their products more accessible to the blind.

Here is an opportunity for individuals with for-profit business management experience to help the nonprofit organizations they are associated with. They can expand their doing-good programs by developing additional funds and expanding the visibility and exposure of their programs.

Franchise Zone
Entrepreneur Media Inc.
2445 McCabe Way
Irvine, CA 92614
(949) 261-2325
entrepreneur.com/
  franzone

73

Franchise Zone
Entrepreneur Magazine

Franchising can be a good way to get into your own business; it can also be a good way to lose money. Franchise Zone can help reduce the risks.

For more than twenty years *Entrepreneur* magazine has been the voice of franchising, bringing comprehensive coverage of the trends, companies, leaders and franchisees that have made this industry a force to be reckoned with.

With the introduction of the Franchise Zone, *Entrepreneur* has launched the most comprehensive franchise resource on the Internet. This new site combines editorial and research resources with Web experience to offer prospective investors the easiest way to find the information they're seeking.

You can access all the franchise coverage from *Entrepreneur* magazine, plus news and content you won't find anywhere else in print or on the Web. Updated on a daily basis, the Franchise Zone is your one-stop shop for the latest and most thorough information you need about franchising.

74

Expense Reduction
Analysts (Franchise)

*Expense Reduction Analysts is a representative sample of many
consulting services franchises available.*

Expense Reduction Analysts purports to be "the world's leading cost management consultancy, operating in fifteen countries for ten years." They help all
types of businesses, small and large, private and public, save money on everyday
operating costs.

The firm was established in 1983 with the aim of helping clients keep costs
down and profits up. Expense Reduction Analysts works with clients to enhance
the value they receive from suppliers simply by using the time, expertise and specialist knowledge and negotiation skills necessary to track and control costs such
as travel, telecommunications, office supplies, printing, couriers, document stor-
age, cleaning, maintenance and more which may not be cost effective for clients
to review internally.

Associates of Expense Reduction Analysts are trained where to look and use
the firm's experiences and worldwide databases of supplier pricing information to
benchmark clients' costs.

They stake their reputation by offering a unique 'no savings, no fee' service—guaranteeing that Expense Reduction Analysts delivers savings to their
clients.

75

Intelligent Office (Franchise)

Executive suite operations are growing in popularity as more individuals start their own small businesses. Intelligent Office is an example of a franchise in this field.

The Intelligent Office is a new concept in executive suites. Available full-time or part-time as a back-up receptionist, the Intelligent Office is a smart new way to have an office. It's also one of the smartest business-to-business franchising concepts around.

Their Remote Receptionist professional phone reception is smart and affordable. Whether you're an office with dozens of employees or a home office that needs to be more professional, The Remote Receptionist can be the best receptionist you've ever had.

As an Intelligent Office franchisee you can help professionals of all kinds to work smarter and more affordably than ever before, creating a win/win situation for them and for you.

The total investment is about $500,000; minimum net worth $1,000,000.

76

Entrepreneur's Source
(Franchise)

*The Entrepreneur's Source is a franchise operation that helps others
find the franchise opportunity that is right for them.*

The Entrepreneur's Source franchisors claim to "provide all our clients with the
most comprehensive, objective, unbiased and meaningful advice available anywhere." They apply their "win-win" principles to four key service areas: educating
individuals in business ownership opportunities; coaching them through the evaluation of their goals and the attainment of their dreams; and guiding them
through career transitions.

They can help individuals evaluate the potential for franchising in their established business, then assist them through business planning, financing, marketing and more. Candidates who have worked with The Entrepreneur's Source are
better informed and better qualified for franchise ownership.

They say that they have helped hundreds of people break the cycle of dependency on employers.

**Case Handyman
Services**
CaseHandyman.com
**House Doctors
Handyman Service**
housedoctors.com
Mr. Handyman
mrhandyman.com

77

Handyman Services

*Home repair is a popular small business for those who enjoy working with
tools and helping to deal with the many problems around the home.
There are a number of franchise operations, or an individual can
create his or her own company.*

A recent *Wall Street Journal* article compared the services of three franchise home
handyman services: Case Handyman Services, with about fifty locations in
twenty-four states; Mr. Handyman, with 140 locations in thirty-five states; and
House Doctors Handyman Service with 200 locations in forty-three states.

These and other companies are attempting to professionalize the business by
establishing these franchise operations. The push comes as America's housing
stock is aging; the average home is now thirty-two years old. And getting good help
is increasingly difficult.

The article concluded that a customer's experience was very much dependent
on the individual doing the work. Hourly rates are about $90—$100 per hour, plus
"trip fees."

The benefits of joining a franchise system include processes and systems, networking, and support from area experts. These are just a few of the key areas that a
franchisor will stress to a prospective franchisee. They will typically guide you
through from pre-opening to grand opening and beyond to ensure that you get off to
the right start.

78

Goddard School (Franchise)

There is a growing view that preschool experience is an important base for childhood development. The Goddard School franchise is one way to get into this growing field.

The Goddard School is a franchise operation for early childhood development. It was recently named the "#1 Franchise Preschool Chain in the United States," by *Entrepreneur* magazine for the third consecutive year (January 2004) and one of the top fifty worldwide "Up and Comers," by *Franchise Times*.

Goddard Systems, Inc. (GSI) is expanding The Goddard School network throughout the United States. Headquartered in King of Prussia, Pennsylvania, GSI currently licenses 160+ franchised schools in twenty-two states.

Franchise opportunities are available nationwide, including newly approved locations in: Boston, Chicago, Dallas, Minneapolis, and North Denver.

The Goddard School offers the foundation to encourage a child's lifelong love of learning. In their warm, loving atmosphere caring teachers support the healthy development of a child from six weeks to six years old. The year round program offers the family the choice of either a half- or full-day schedule.

Goddard Developmental Guidelines form the basis of special lesson plans that are brought to life in a fun and imaginative way. Learning centers for dramatic play, creative art, science, quiet reading, and blocks and puzzles provide the child the opportunity to explore independently and confidently.

Special Travel, Adventure

$\mathcal{T}$ravel is one of the activities that we all look forward to as we cut down on our full-time careers. Once we have done the popular cruises and country tours, the challenge is to find those trips and travel adventures that provide special challenges and insights and that we did not have time for earlier.

Explore The World In Depth

One of the ways of making travel more of a life experience is to go into depth in a country or region with respect to the area's history, its people, its geography, its language and the other things that make it special. In short, to become an expert on a different part of the world.

Get To Know Others

A number of the ideas presented relate to interpersonal involvement with people in other parts of the world. What better way than to visit with them in their homes and then hosting them in yours?

The following are some starting points for finding some special ways to expand your vistas or to get special enjoyment from those areas that you are already familiar with.

Elderhostel
75 Federal Street
Boston, MA
02110-1941
elderhostel.org

79

Elderhostel

Elderhostel is a not-for-profit organization that provides exceptional travel and learning adventures to nearly 200,000 older adults each year.

Elderhostel was founded as a not-for-profit organization in 1975 by two collaborators—Marty Knowlton, a world traveling, free spirited, social activist and former educator, and David Bianco, a highly organized university administrator. Knowlton had recently returned from a four-year walking tour of Europe, carrying only a backpack of bare essentials and staying in youth hostels. He was impressed by the youth hostel concept, with its safe, inexpensive lodgings and opportunities to meet fellow travelers.

Knowlton was also taken with institutions in Scandinavia, called folk schools. There, he saw older adults handing down age-old traditions—folk art, music, lore and dance—to younger generations. Seeing Europeans in their sixties, seventies and eighties playing an active and positive role in their communities made Knowlton wonder why their American counterparts didn't have a similar opportunity to remain active after retirement. Why not give them continued opportunities to learn as well?

Elderhostel believes learning is a lifelong pursuit that opens minds and enriches lives. Their participants come from every walk of life to learn together, to exchange ideas, and to explore the world.

Nearly 10,000 programs are offered each year in about 100 countries. Service programs are between one and four weeks in length, and include historical preservation, museum curation, conservation work at national and state parks, environmental research, archaeology, education projects, and construction of affordable housing.

Offerings include educational trips, college and university-based Institutes for Learning in Retirement, and Elderhostel Service Programs, engaging teams of hostelers in short-term volunteer projects in the United States and around the world.

**National Geographic
Expeditions**
(888) 966-8687
nationalgeographic.com/
ngexpeditions

80

National
Geographic Expeditions

*Long respected for its presentation of remote parts of the world,
National Geographic now offers travel to many of those places.*

National Geographic Expeditions brings you "the world and all that's in it"—with the peace of mind that comes from traveling with an organization that has been exploring our planet and discovering its wonders for more than a century.

Track gray whales in the Sea of Cortez; ride an elephant up to the hilltop Amber Fort of Jaipur; view ancient Inca mummies alongside the Society-funded archaeologist who made the discoveries.

Travel not as an observer but as an active participant, with boundless chances to be surrounded by natural wonders and exotic wildlife, to explore celebrated archaeological sites and important antiquities, to learn about different cultures and environments, and to meet local people and share in their traditions.

Expeditions are crafted with *National Geographic* experts to create one-of-a-kind adventures that incorporate the insights, knowledge, and passion of those who know the destinations intimately. *National Geographic*'s name opens doors worldwide, providing access to special events, to scientific installations, to archaeological digs, and to private homes.

Whenever possible, visits are arranged to Society-sponsored research sites so you can meet the scientists whose discoveries you've read about in the pages of *National Geographic* magazine.

81

Outward Bound

Outward Bound offers challenging adventure-based experiences in wilderness schools.

With over forty years of experience, Outward Bound USA, a national nonprofit educational organization, is dedicated to helping people build internal fortitude and confidence through personal achievement.

Outward Bound excels in its long-standing tradition of using the wilderness as a "classroom" for self discovery and with over a half a million alumni, their programs have touched the lives of more people than ever before.

Outward Bound's wilderness programs will take you to some of the most beautiful and untouched wilderness areas in the U.S., where you can enjoy a wide range of activities including sailing, backpacking, whitewater rafting, sea kayaking, rock climbing and dog sledding. Over 750 expeditions, ranging in length from four days to three months, are offered year-round and available for people of all ages.

Outward Bound was first conceived in Great Britain during World War II and brought to the United States in the early 1950's. Based on the philosophies of renowned educator Kurt Hahn, the programs today work to instill self esteem, self-reliance, concern for others and care for the environment.

In addition to the expansive wilderness programs, Outward Bound delivers adventure and challenge in the urban setting, in workrooms and classrooms to help people achieve possibilities and to inspire them to serve others and care for the world around them.

CEDAM International
One Fox Road
Croton-on-Hudson, NY
 10520
(914) 271-5365
cedam.org

82

CEDAM International

CEDAM stands for Conservation, Education, Diving, Awareness and Marine research. It provides marine diving expeditions throughout the world.

CEDAM International is a not-for-profit organization founded in 1967. The organization is dedicated to the understanding, protection and preservation of the world's marine resources.

Through their expeditions, CEDAM International volunteer divers actively participate in scientific research and conservation-oriented education projects. The results of their findings and efforts are disseminated to both the scientific and lay communities.

CEDAM International expeditioners are novice and experienced divers, explorers, underwater videographers and photographers, and amateur and skilled naturalists. Expeditions are led by professional researchers and scientists.

Past years have taken the organization around the world to: Galapagos, Mexico, Venezuela, Honduras, Seychelles, Red Sea, Kenya Coast, Australia, Belize, Bahamas, Cayman Islands, Solomon Islands, Costa Rica, Fiji, and Tahiti.

Earthwatch International
3 Clock Tower Place, Suite 100
Maynard, MA 01754
(800) 776-0188
earthwatch.org

83

Earthwatch Institute

Earthwatch Institute engages people worldwide in scientific field research and education to promote the understanding and action necessary for a sustainable environment.

Earthwatch is an international nonprofit organization, founded in Boston and now with offices in Oxford, England; Melbourne, Australia; and Tokyo, Japan.

50,000 members and supporters are spread across the U.S., Europe, Africa, Asia and Australia. 3,500 of their members volunteer their time and skills to work with 120 research scientists each year on Earthwatch field research projects in over fifty countries all around the world.

They believe that decision-making involving these research issues not only requires objective scientific data from the field, but must engage the general public through active participation in the scientific process if it is to become widely accepted and effective.

Unlike other environmental organizations, Earthwatch Institute puts people in the field where they can assist scientists in their field work. They are part of the action, they learn new skills, and develop a deeper understanding of their role in building a sustainable future. They believe that teaching and promoting scientific literacy is the best way to systematically approach and solve the many complex environmental and social issues facing society today.

Earthwatch acts as a catalyst and a liaison among the scientific community, conservation and environmental organizations, policy makers, business, and the general public. They place a strong emphasis on producing sound results and much of their work is accomplished in collaboration with conservation and education non-government organizations and local host country partners.

Where do you want to go to make a difference?

84

Sierra Club Outings

The Sierra Club offers a variety of outdoor adventures, from backpacking to global trekking for people of all ages.

With over 100 years of wilderness travel experience, and as a part of the largest grassroots organization in the Country, Sierra Club Outings offers over 350 trips annually to unique destinations around the world.

They provide a variety of quality outdoor adventures—from backpacking to family trips to global trekking—for people of all ages and abilities.

They offer six reasons to travel with them: (1) More than 100 years of wilderness travel experience, coupled with a rich outdoor history, (2) Over 350 trips around the world, providing a variety of activities and destinations, (3) Chances to explore the world with other environmentally conscious individuals, (4) Small group sizes, giving you the benefit of a more intimate vacation experience, (5) Skilled and friendly volunteer trip staff who donate their time out of a love for the land, and (6) Opportunities to learn about conservation, natural history, and wildlife.

Trip brochures are available on the Sierra Club website.

85

Over The Hill Gang

Over the Hill Gang International
1820 W. Colorado Ave.
Colorado Springs, CO
80904
(719) 389-0022
othgi.com

Over The Hill Gang International provides unsurpassed camaraderie, outstanding discounts and great trips for people fifty and over.

The Over The Hill Gang are enthusiastic, fun-loving people who enjoy sharing the experience of skiing and other outdoor activities with other physically active seniors. Membership is available to individuals and to couples as long as one spouse is at least fifty.

More than 6,000 people in the U.S. and around the world enjoy OTHG membership. Benefits of membership include: deep discounts at U.S. & Canadian ski areas; camaraderie on trips and regular ski days at many resorts—including Vail, Breckenridge and Keystone; great U.S. and international skiing in the winter; bicycling, hiking, golfing and whitewater rafting adventures in the summer and fall.

Regular publications like the quarterly newsletter "The Legend," the Trip Catalog with details for OTHG trips and an annual benefits directory, listing 300+ discounts are available to members.

As an OTHG member, you may want to join the activities provided by local chapters by becoming a chapter member as well. Chapter membership is optional. Local chapters are run by volunteers and offer more opportunities to see your OTHG friends on regular ski days, social occasions, weekend events, and even week-long ski trips.

**Work Your Way
Around The World**
Vacation Work
9 Park End Street,
Oxford England
vacationwork.co.uk

86

Work Your Way
Around The World

*For the really ambitious retirees, who want to combine travel with the opportunity
to really get to know people in other parts of the world, are willing
to combine manual or intellectual labor with their travel, and want to help
pay for the trips, working your way around the world is worth exploring.*

The bible for exploring work/travel opportunities is *Work Your Way Around the World*, by Susan Griffith. It was first published in 1983 in the UK and has been revised every other year since. It has a European bias, and is quite current.

The book provides information on preparation, getting a job before you go or after you get there, rewards and risks, and ways to work for your passage. It describes a number of types of jobs that are possible, and then goes into detail about the various regulations and limitations related to specific countries.

The author, Susan Griffith, who is based in Cambridge, England, began her guidebook in 1980. Since then the world of travel has changed dramatically, and the opportunities to work in a foreign country have been affected by a number of factors, including the concern about terrorists, the evolution of the European Common Market, and the economics of the travel industry itself.

She warns that the fact finding for Americans will be different than that of the British counterparts because the U.S. is not part of the European Union. Getting a work permit will prove difficult, and sometimes the best jobs can be had without one.

The good news about the book is that it is crammed full of information in its 576 pages. The bad news is that the print is quite small and can be a burden to read it all.

87

Backpacking
For Seniors

**Lonely Planet
Publications**
lonelyplanet.com
**Federation of
International Youth
Travel Organizations**
fiyto.org

*A growing number of retirees are hitting the trail with the
younger generations of backpackers.*

Since the 1980's, a network of guesthouses, hostels and budget-travel agencies has sprung up around the world, luring adventure-loving retirees. The following are two sources of information on creating your own adventure.

Lonely Planet Publications: A budget-travel publisher of guides for places off the beaten track has created an 'Older Travelers' chat room, subtitled "spend the kids' inheritance and hit the road." Book your stay at one of over 4,000 hostels worldwide in only a few clicks. With real-time reservations, secure technology, informative write-ups, and color pictures, you will wonder how you ever planned a trip before using Hostelworld.

In addition to backpacking, choose from over 200 unique small group journeys, adventures and expeditions to every continent on earth. Discover inspirational trekking, cycling, climbing, paddling, cruising, touring, camel riding or special interest adventures.

Federation of International Youth Travel Organizations, Copenhagen: The Federation of International Youth Travel Organizations is the world's only membership association and trade forum for youth travel professionals. Based in Copenhagen, it provides the pre-eminent professional forum to exchange information and advance the interests of the young traveler.

FIYTO is a member of the World Tourism Organization (WTO) and the Pacific Asia Travel Association (PATA). FIYTO enjoys operational relations with the United Nations Educational, Scientific and Cultural Organization (UNESCO).

Although focused on the youth market, they are a source of contacts with the hostel and backpacking travel industry. They have been instrumental in organizing the Global Work Experience Association.

Hostelling International-USA
8401 Colesville Road,
 Suite 600
Silver Spring, MD
 20910
(301) 495-1240
hiayh.org

88

American Youth Hostel
Hostelling International USA

While focused on youth, seniors are becoming a significant element in the hostelling experience.

American Youth Hostel is the American affiliate of the Hostelling International network of more than 5,000 hostels in over sixty countries. As a nonprofit organization, they have nearly seventy years of experience serving travelers.

Hostelling International USA (registered as American Youth Hostels, Inc.) is a nonprofit membership organization founded in 1934 to promote international understanding of the world and its people through hostelling. HI-USA operates a network of more than 100 hostel accommodations throughout the United States that are inexpensive, safe and clean. Hostels range from urban high-rise buildings with hundreds of beds to small hostels in rural settings.

HI-USA, in cooperation with other worldwide national associations, belongs to the International Youth Hostel Federation (IYHF). Hostelling International USA and the blue triangle with the tree and hut are the trademark and seal of approval of the IYHF, assuring travelers quality, affordable accommodations and travel programs worldwide.

HI-USA is also associated with thirty-four councils throughout the United States. These councils provide local members and visitors with a wide range of special programs, events, trips and activities.

89

Hospitality Club

Hospitality Club is a network of individuals who help each other when traveling.

The aim of the Hospitality Club is to bring people together—hosts and guests, travelers and locals. Thousands of Hospitality Club members around the world help each other when they are traveling—be it with a roof for the night or a guided tour through town. Joining is very simple, takes just a minute and everyone is welcome.

Members can look at each other's profiles, send messages and post comments about their experience on the website.

The club is supported by volunteers who believe in one idea: by bringing travelers in touch with people in the place they visit, and by giving "locals" a chance to meet people from other cultures they can increase intercultural understanding and strengthen the peace on our planet.

Participants can meet friendly people and find free accommodation when traveling to any corner of the world.

There are no obligations (you do not have to host anyone at your home!), membership is free and they would love to have you in their world wide web of friendly people.

International Home Exchange Network
118 Flamingo Avenue
Daytona Beach, FL
 32118
(386) 238-3633
ihen.com

90

International Home Exchange

An opportunity to share your home or vacation spot in exchange for experiencing other parts of the world on an inexpensive basis.

The International Home Exchange Network, the first website devoted to the listing of home exchanges and private rentals, recently celebrated its tenth anniversary on the Internet.

IHEN has served the needs of the International traveler for over nine years. Thousands of members have safely and successfully avoided hotel and restaurant bills; obtained free use of cars and boats; and lived like a resident apart from commercial tourist attractions.

On the web, IHEN has enjoyed unparalleled success and become a popular destination for "surfers" worldwide. It has averaged 350,000 file requests per month from over seventy countries.

The International Home Exchange Network has been selected by New Riders in its "World Wide Web Top 1000" and rated by Pointcom among the top five percent of all websites currently on the Internet.

91

Seniors Vacation
and Home Exchange

*Another exchange network, with emphasis on sharing with others in the
over-fifty crowd and including more than housing.*

The Seniors Vacation and Home Exchange is the only vacation and home exchange exclusively for the over-fifty age group.

It provides great value and many more vacation options than other Internet home exchange programs.

It allows you to do a straight vacation exchange of your home. Or, if you prefer, exchange hospitality vacations. You visit with them and, in return, they visit with you.

Seniors Vacation and Home Exchange is not confined to houses or second homes. It allows you to exchange your motor home or boat, and to list non-exchange commercial or private accommodations.

turkeytravelplanner.com
newenglandtravelplanner.com
guidetocaribbeanvacations.com

92

On Line
Travel Guidebooks

A new approach to getting up-to-date and in-depth travel information on the Internet.

For the most up-to-date travel information, check out the new guidebooks being presented directly on the Internet. Most of them are free, and they are updated almost daily.

One of these new websites is turkeytravelplanner.com, written and updated by Tom Brosnahan. His hardcopy guidebooks have totaled 800 pages or more; the website is 1,400 pages.

His Turkey Travel Planner differs from the books in several ways. It is updated daily, it is heavily illustrated, it has message boards and forums, it is full of cultural and historical information, and it is organized in terms of the basic questions that most travelers will ask in advance of a trip to Turkey.

Brosnahan is also developing newenglandtravelplanner.com, and one of his associates, M. Timothy O'Keefe is operating guidetocaribbeanvacations.com.

93

International Fund For Animal Welfare

International Fund for Animal Welfare
411 Main Street
Yarmouth Port, MA
02675
(508) 744-2000
ifaw.org

Travel to exotic places of the world with a purpose—
helping to promote animal welfare.

The IFAW works to improve the welfare of wild and domestic animals throughout the world by reducing the commercial exploitation of animals, protecting wildlife habitats and assisting animals in distress. They seek to motivate the public to prevent cruelty to animals and to promote animal welfare and conservation policies that advance the well-being of both animals and people.

From the outset, the founders of the International Fund for Animal Welfare rejected the notion that the interests of humans and animals were separate. Instead they embraced the understanding that the fate and future of harp seals—and all other animals on Earth—are inextricably linked to our own.

IFAW begins its fourth decade of operation with more than 200 experienced campaigners, legal and political experts, and internationally acclaimed scientists working from offices in thirteen countries around the world.

They are now joined in this important work by some two million contributors worldwide. This broad base of support makes it possible for IFAW to engage communities, government leaders, and like-minded organizations around the world and achieve lasting solutions to pressing animal welfare and conservation challenges—solutions that benefit both animals and people.

IFAW can be a starting point to find volunteering opportunities in the animal welfare field.

**Wildlife Conservation
Society**
Bronx Zoo
New York, NY
wcs.org

94

Wildlife
Conservation Society

*The world's wildlife needs you—and through WCS you can personally
join the fight to save wild creatures and wild lands around the globe.*

The Wildlife Conservation Society saves wildlife and wild lands through careful science, international conservation, education, and the management of the world's largest system of urban wildlife parks.

These activities change attitudes toward nature and help people imagine wildlife and humans living in sustainable interaction on both a local and a global scale.

WCS owns and operates animal collections. Since 1895, WCS has worked from its New York based Bronx Zoo headquarters to save wildlife and wild lands throughout the world.

They combine the resources of wildlife parks in New York with field projects around the globe to inspire care for nature, provide leadership in environmental education, and help sustain our planet's biological diversity.

Today WCS is at work in fifty-three nations across Africa, Asia, Latin America and North America, protecting wild landscapes that are home to a vast variety of species from butterflies to tigers.

At the WCS website you can find out how you can help wildlife species or conservation projects, volunteer your time, and choose a career helping wildlife.

Healthcare, Medicine

The high cost of healthcare is a major problem, not just for seniors but for society as a whole. As people live longer (largely due to the wonderful medications and treatments that are being developed and regularly improved), there are more of them to be supported by the younger generations. No one wants to reverse the trend toward better health, but we would like to find some ways to reduce the associated costs.

How can we become more knowledgeable about our own healthcare, the medicine we take, and the ways that we can reduce our healthcare costs by staying in better health? Are there trade-offs that we should be aware of, so that we don't spend our last dollars on approaches that may give us only a few months more?

Becoming more involved in the process, helping others with their healthcare solutions, and focusing on specific health conditions that affect one personally are excellent ways to find enrichment and help yourself and society.

The suggestions presented here are just starting points. For each idea, there are hundreds of others that you might pursue. It's never too late to get smarter and become better masters of our own fate.

95

Healthcare Opportunities Begin At Home

There is a wide range of opportunities in the area of healthcare and medicine for individuals who want to become active and provide a significant contribution to society.

One of the most direct ways to reduce the cost of healthcare is to help ourselves and others to stay healthy. People are living longer, due to improved medication and healthcare practices, but most of all due to the fact that people are taking better care of themselves.

Helping others take better care of themselves is one area of opportunity for the active retiree. Getting your family, friends and neighbors to eat healthier foods and to exercise more can go a long way to reduce obesity, a major reducer of life span and, maybe more important, a major impediment to the quality of that life.

The most effective cure for containing the escalating cost of healthcare begins with the individual. If we take a hard look at the kinds of food we put in our shopping carts, how often we eat at the fast-food outlets and how much exercise we get, we will see where the problem and the solution lie.

We can take action to serve as a model, and to help our families, our friends and our neighbors to take personal responsibility to live a healthy life. This will result in less reliance on expensive medical care, and expecting the government to take care of us.

Just one example of the information and motivation that is available on the Internet is the WalkingWorks.com site provided by the Blue Cross Blue Shield Association. It presents a program of walking, which can help one lose weight, lower cholesterol, strengthen the heart, and reduce the likelihood of serious health problems down the road.

We can live longer, happier lives and reduce the cost to the younger generations.

Archives of Internal Medicine
archinte.ama-assn.org
American Pharmacists Association
aphanet.org
National Institute on Drug Abuse
nida.nih.gov

96

Pharmacy Maven

An increasing number of studies underscore the need for more vigilance by physicians about the drugs they are prescribing, particularly for elderly people.

A study at Duke University found that about twenty-one percent of elderly patients had filled prescriptions for drugs that are known to cause harm or induce harmful side effects in those over sixty-five.

A recent article in the AARP Bulletin featured a pharmacist who has developed a major business of reviewing the various medications being taken by seniors in nursing homes and assisted living facilities. He found that seniors were being over-prescribed and taking medications that had potentially dangerous interactions with other drugs they were taking. He is one of a few thousand consultant pharmacists nationwide who specialize in identifying, resolving and preventing medication-related problems that affect, and afflict, older people.

The larger pharmacies are now providing information on potentially harmful interactions among prescriptions they handle for customers. However, computer systems that are fully effective have yet to be developed, and many people go to several different pharmacies, including online services, to save money or for convenience.

Helping seniors to understand the potential problems associated with the medications their doctors prescribe, or at least helping them find appropriate resources to give them that assistance, can be a rewarding avocation, or perhaps even a vocation for you. The information gained will be helpful in protecting yourself, your family members and others close to you.

97

Researching Medical Options

Schine On-line Services Inc.
findcure.com
The HealthResource Inc.
thehealthresource.com
Doctor Evidence
doctorevidence.com

Many people become experts in healthcare options when they or close friends have medical problems

When patients begin the process of getting advice from their doctors or other healthcare specialists, they may become confused because of too much information, or unhappy because they cannot get the responses they believe they should be getting.

The Internet is an excellent place to start in doing research, but typically the amount and variety of information over the Internet can be overwhelming.

Gary Schine, of Providence, R.I. started a business of sorting through the various options when he was told that he would die from a rare form of leukemia because there was no cure. Through his own research he was able to find a clinical trial in San Diego in which he participated; he has been in remission since completing the experimental treatment. He feels he owes his cure to his own efforts in researching and finding the latest information on treating his illness—a newly developed treatment that his doctor knew nothing about.

Other services like Gary's can help in sorting out the options, which can be overwhelming. There is no single consumer organization that pulls information together, comparing drug effectiveness, treatment options and quality of medical care for a patient's specific condition. It can be difficult to separate fact from fiction, and truth from advertising.

Above are some of the companies that do medical research for patients. An alternative to using these services is to do what Gary Schine did, do the research yourself, and perhaps find a calling in the medical research field.

Help of Ojai
111 W. Santa Ana St.
Ojai, CA 93023
(805) 646-5122
helpofojai.org

98

Lower Cost
Medication Help

*A retired grandmother in Ojai, California is helping other seniors
find cheaper prescription drugs on the Internet.*

This thoughtful and caring woman has helped dozens of low-income people cut their drug bills by steering them to bargains in Canada, where socialized health care keeps prices low and the exchange rate favors Americans.

Dogged by an array of medical problems herself, including an advancing case of glaucoma that may soon leave her blind, the sixty-nine year-old doesn't buy her own drugs online. She gets by on her Social Security check, and her HMO covers most of her medicines.

But she took on the volunteer work for Help of Ojai, a local nonprofit group anyway, because drug prices "are just terrible," and she is tired of waiting for Congress to do something about it. She helps people who are intimidated by computers or worried that they will be taken in by unscrupulous operators. She consults only pharmacies she has verified as licensed by the Canadian government.

One recent experience was helping a caller who was spending nearly $300 for a thirty-day supply of Actonel. She was able to find a Canadian supplier at a ninety day savings of $754.

If taking on a project like this in your community is appealing, contact Help of Ojai to learn more about their experience in this and their other programs.

The Senior Initiative
636 Washington Street,
Suite 5
Canton, MA 02021
(781) 821-0868
theseniorinitiative.org

99

Fighting High Drug Costs
The Senior Initiative

If you are concerned about the high cost of medications, you can become active with a group that is dedicated to reducing the cost of those drugs.

The Senior Initiative was founded by an individual who was upset about the fact that AARP supported the Medicare Prescription Drug Improvement and Modernization Act of 2003. He felt that this was a betrayal of thirty-five million AARP members, giving Congress the political cover it needed to pass a badly flawed bill.

In Senior Initiative's view, AARP sold out to the drug and insurance industries. The goal of the new organization is to become an alternative force in the discussion of the critical issues of the day that affect the health and financial security of all older Americans.

They plan to avoid the inherent conflicts that arise when, as they see it, an organization such as AARP depends upon the sale of insurance and prescription drugs to its members for a large share of its revenue. The Senior Initiative will be a watchdog group whose mission is to keep Congress and AARP honest and focused on the needs of seniors.

They invite all seniors to join. As the new organization grows and takes shape, it will have numerous opportunities for volunteers.

LABioMed
1124 W. Carson Street
Torrance, CA 90502
(310) 222-2820
LABioMed.org

100

L.A. Biomedical
Research Institute

Many research organizations can use the help of experienced business executives and professionals.

Service on their boards or in other capacities helps the institutions and gives the individuals insights into the latest developments.

For individuals interested in becoming more involved in healthcare and the state of the art in medical research, an involvement with a leading medical research institute can provide a great deal of satisfaction and the opportunity to be close to leading experts in a number of fields.

The Los Angeles Biomedical Research Institute is an example of a leading institution with a variety of diseases under their purview. LABioMed conducts biomedical research, provides education and training of scientists, and provides a variety of community services such as nutritional assistance, childhood immunization, anti-violence programs and various disease education initiatives.

Located in Los Angeles County on the campus of Harbor-UCLA Medical Center, LA BioMed is a freestanding, not-for-profit biomedical research, training and service organization. It is an affiliate of both the UCLA School of Medicine and the Harbor-UCLA Medical Center, and has an annual budget of $58 million. It has a faculty of nearly 200 investigators and a total employment of 1,000 full- and part-time people.

The Institute is also well-known for its training of scientists and physician scientists and a variety of community service functions. Contact LABioMed to find out about opportunities to become active with their Foundation and various committees. They may be helpful in finding a similar institution in your area.

**National Institutes
of Health**
9000 Rockville Pike
Bethesda, MD 20892
(301) 496-4000
nih.gov

101

National Institutes
of Health

*An excellent place to start for those interested in learning more about
healthcare and medical research is the National Institutes of Health.*

NIH is the steward of medical and behavioral research for the Nation, an Agency
under the U.S. Department of Health and Human Services. Headquartered in
Bethesda, Maryland, NIH funds scientific studies at universities and research
institutions across the Nation.

The NIH comprises the Office of the Director and twenty-seven Institutes and
Centers. The Office of the Director is responsible for setting policy for NIH and for
planning, managing, and coordinating the programs and activities of all NIH
components.

Begun as a one-room Laboratory of Hygiene in 1887, the National Institutes
of Health today is one of the world's foremost medical research centers.

The mission of NIH is science in pursuit of fundamental knowledge about the
nature and behavior of living systems, and the application of that knowledge to
extend healthy life and reduce the burdens of illness and disability.

A visit to their website will open many doors to the status of research throughout the Country and to possible ways for you to help.

**National Institutes
of Health**
clinicaltrials.gov

102

Clinical Trials

*With a new service on the Internet, individuals can now obtain
current information on thousands of clinical trials in all types of
diseases and medications.*

Individuals who have an interest in a specific disease, whether it is because they have it, or someone close to them does, probably want to learn as much as they can about that disease and what is being done about it. One very important resource is the website clinicaltrials.gov, supported by the National Institutes of Health.

Clinicaltrials.gov offers up-to-date information for locating Federally and privately supported clinical trials for a wide range of diseases and conditions. A 'clinical trial' (or clinical research) is a research study involving human volunteers to answer specific health questions. 'Interventional trials' determine whether experimental treatments or new ways of using known therapies are safe and effective under controlled environments. 'Observational trials' address health issues in large groups of people or populations in natural settings.

Clinicaltrials.gov currently contains approximately 11,700 clinical studies sponsored by the National Institutes of Health, other Federal agencies, and private industry. Studies listed in the database are conducted in all fifty states and in over ninety countries. Clinicaltrials.gov receives over 2.5 million page views per month and hosts approximately 16,000 visitors daily.

You can search by disease name, by category of disease, and by condition. Searching under polycythemia vera as an example, seventeen studies were found, each of them still recruiting for participants.

For each study, you can find out who is doing it, the purpose of the study, criteria for eligibility to participate and complete contact information.

103

Samaritan House Clinic

**Samaritan House
Medical Center**
117 North San Mateo
Drive
San Mateo, CA 94401
(650) 347-1556
samaritanhouse.com

*Many free clinics have been established, and many more are needed.
They can use your help.*

Samaritan House Clinic is just one example. It is affiliated with Samaritan House, a nonprofit agency located in San Mateo, California, providing services to low-income individuals.

The clinic offers free health care to local residents who have no health insurance, through a group of over fifty volunteer doctors, dentists, nurses, and pharmacists; two paid physicians; and a steady stream of University of California at San Francisco medical students and residents who receive part of their training at the clinic.

Even if you are not a trained medical specialist, you can help organize such a service in your community, by enlisting the support of the doctors, nurses and other specialists that might be needed.

Volunteers in Medicine
15 Northridge Drive
Hilton Head Island, SC
 29925
(843) 681-6612
hiltonheadisland.com/vim

104

Volunteers
in Medicine

Volunteers in Medicine is another example of free clinics needing your help.

Volunteers in Medicine clinics provide free medical and dental service to families and individuals who otherwise have no access to health care. The clinics are staffed by retired medical professionals, other volunteers, and a small number of paid staff.

Founded in Hilton Head, South Carolina, clinics now operate in Pennsylvania, Florida, Indiana, and elsewhere. More than 100 medical professionals (doctors, dentists, nurses and other specialists) living in the area donate their services to the Clinic.

These volunteer medical personnel are augmented by currently practicing professionals who have indicated a desire to contribute their time and donate their services to the VIM Clinic.

Community volunteers are a critical and significant factor in the success of the Volunteers In Medicine Clinic. The VIM volunteers are considered "partners in care" as they greet patients and escort them through the patient care process, offer explanations of the Clinic procedures and services and let the patients know that someone hears their problems and cares about them as individuals.

Community volunteers also supply operational and administrative support to the staff. Maybe you can help organize a similar program in your area.

105

Hospital Volunteers

Angels in the ER
St. John's Health Center
Santa Monica, CA
**American Society of
Directors of
Voluntee**r **Services**
asdvs.org

There are many ways to help patients and staffs at local hospitals.
This is just one example.

Angels in the ER, a volunteer service at St. John's Health Center in Santa Monica, California, was founded by a nurse who ran the employee health office. She was disturbed that patients had to sit and wait for hours with few updates on their status.

The group now has more than thirty adult volunteers filling four-hour shifts seven days a week giving patients and their loved ones a lot of attention. The hospital's emergency department had often fielded written complaints about long waits and inattention to visitors, but since the Angels in the ER took the floor more than four years ago, the letters have dwindled to a handful a year.

Every hospital has similar sets of problems; the professional staffs are busy focusing on delivering medical care. Volunteers can provide TLC, information and attention that might otherwise be in short supply.

To find information on how you can help start a volunteer service in your hospital, contact that hospital's administrator. For additional information, contact the American Society of Directors of Volunteer Services at their website.

Community

Charity begins at home. Helping others in our own cities or communities has a direct impact on our own well-being and contentment. If we have problems in our neighborhood, do we help solve them, or flee? If our neighbors need help, we help them.

Community help can take on many forms. It can be as simple as bringing in the newspaper for the vacationing family next door, to heading up the annual Fourth of July picnic, to planting new trees along Elm Street.

The following are examples of activities that were started by someone. You may want to participate in some of these programs, do something similar in your community, or come up with a newly conceived project of your own.

106

Neighborhood Watch

*One of the most direct ways to help your community,
your neighbors and your own home.*

The Neighborhood Watch Program, an initiative within Citizen Corps, is a highly successful effort that has been in existence for more than thirty years in cities and counties across America. It provides a specialized infrastructure that brings together local officials, law enforcement and citizens to protect our communities.

Around the Country, neighbors for decades have banded together to create Neighborhood Watch programs. They understand that the active participation of neighborhood residents is a critical element in community safety—not through vigilantism, but simply through a willingness to look out for suspicious activity in their neighborhood, and report that activity to law enforcement and to each other.

In the aftermath of September 11, 2001, the need for strengthening and securing our communities has become even more critical, and Neighborhood Watch groups have taken on greater significance.

In addition to serving a crime prevention role, Neighborhood Watch can also be used as the basis for bringing neighborhood residents together to focus on disaster preparedness as well as terrorism awareness.

If you have a Neighborhood Watch program in your community, get involved. If not, help get one started.

Rebuilding Together
1536 Sixteenth Street NW
Washington, DC
20036-1042
(800) 4 REHAB 9
rebuildingtogether.com

107

Rebuilding Together

*Rebuilding Together is another program working to help people
repair their homes and the elderly to 'age in place.'*

Neighbors helping neighbors, like the barn-raising of old, is the American spirit in action. Rebuilding Together was born of that spirit as people came together to help their low-income neighbors fix their houses—first in Texas, then in Washington, DC, and then California and beyond.

The organization was started in 1988 as "Christmas in April" and the first office was in the basement of a Washington, DC home. The national office assisted in the planning, development and coordination of all services, as well as focusing on replicating the volunteer rehabilitation model in cities and towns across the Nation. Now there are over 250 affiliates nationwide.

In 2000, the organization, recognizing the growing needs of low-income homeowners, expanded its mission to provide more year-round services and a greater diversity of services, all focused around the core goal of rehabilitation and revitalization.

With the expanded mission came a new name, a name that reflects the work of Rebuilding Together and the partnership approach used by the organization.

The new name, Rebuilding Together, also reflects the organization's position in providing solutions to a national crisis by enabling low-income elderly to age in place. Today, Rebuilding Together affiliates provide an array of home rehabilitation services including emergency services, home modifications, weatherization and nonprofit facility repair.

Shelter Partnership, Inc.
523 W. Sixth St., Suite 616
Los Angeles, CA 90014
(213) 688-2188
shelterpartnership.org

108

Shelter Partnership, Inc.

Focused on the Los Angeles area, Shelter Partnership can be a model for individuals in other communities who want to do something about the problem of homelessness.

Shelter Partnership, Inc. is a nonprofit organization that develops resources and housing for the growing number of homeless families and individuals in Los Angeles County.

Since 1985, Shelter Partnership has continued to provide a variety of support to hundreds of agencies, free of charge.

Shelter Partnership also serves as a resource to public agencies, the business community, local and national media, and community members involved in the issues of homelessness and the creation of permanent, affordable housing.

**America's Second
Harvest**
35 E. Wacker Dr.,
 Suite 2000
Chicago, IL 60601
(800) 771-2303
secondharvest.org

109

America's
Second Harvest

*The mission of America's Second Harvest is to create a hunger-free
America, with food banks and food rescue organizations.*

America's Second Harvest volunteers distribute food and grocery products through
a nationwide network of certified affiliates, increase public awareness of domestic
hunger, and advocate for policies that benefit America's hungry.

The network includes more than 200 food banks and food-rescue organizations,
serving every county in the U.S. The effectiveness and operating efficiency of this
network depends on the cooperation of food banks, food rescue organizations, service agencies, donors, and national programs.

Food banks serve people in need by securing and storing surplus food and dis-
tributing it through their own network of local service agencies. Food rescue organizations often operate within a shorter time-frame, picking up and delivering
perishable foods on a single run.

A number of America's Second Harvest affiliates secure and distribute food in
their local community through both of these methods.

Ending hunger in America depends on the volunteer work of millions of Americans who know that they can make a difference. There are as many different ways
to volunteer as there are individuals and communities across this Country.

You can help out in your local community through activities such as helping to
organize, manage and tutor kids at a local Kids Cafe, repackaging donated food for
use at food pantries, or transporting food to charitable agencies and the hungry
people who use their services.

Beyond Shelter, Inc.
520 S. Virgil Ave.,
Suite 200
Los Angeles, CA 90020
(213) 252-0772
beyondshelter.org

110

Beyond
Shelter, Inc.

Beyond Shelter provides services to deal with poverty, homelessness and welfare dependency. Their programs have national as well as local impact.

Founded in 1988, Beyond Shelter's mission is to combat chronic poverty, welfare dependency and homelessness among families with children, through the provision of housing and social services and the promotion of systemic change.

Its goals are: to enhance the quality of life of families, while affirming their autonomy and dignity; to promote programs and methodologies to help families and individuals attain improved economic and social well-being; to promote and develop service-enriched affordable housing for low-income people; and to promote people-centered housing and services delivery in the nonprofit and public sectors through the sharing of information.

The agency's programs in Southern California serve as a laboratory for the development of cutting-edge methodologies, helping to guide the evolution of both social policy and service delivery mechanisms nationwide.

Beyond Shelter currently promotes four main initiatives to address chronic poverty, homelessness and welfare dependency. Each initiative provides a distinct and adaptable methodology, utilizing existing resources in new ways.

The focus of each initiative is to promote systemic change on a national, regional and local scale. This is accomplished primarily through the agency's Institute for Research, Training and Technical Assistance.

Food From The Hood
P.O. Box 8268
Los Angeles, CA 90008
(323) 759-7000
foodfromthehood.com

111

Food From The Hood

Food From The Hood is an example of attracting at-risk young people to the challenges and rewards of entrepreneurial endeavors. It is an opportunity for experienced business people to help their communities by helping young people.

Food From The Hood (FFTH) is the Nation's first student-managed natural food products company. It was created in 1992 in response to the Los Angeles uprising. What started as a classroom project at Crenshaw High School has become a nationally acclaimed program.

FFTH is a unique nonprofit organization dedicated to the empowerment of today's youth through the development of real-world, entrepreneurial training. The program combines work-based skills training, academic tutoring, life skills development and practical business experience working with seasoned entrepreneurs.

The program has been profiled in a number of national media.

The mission of the organization is to foster business, academic, and life skills for youth, impacting the students' ability to become self-sufficient, contributing adults. To date, Food From The Hood has awarded over $140,000 in college scholarships to the student-managers. Seventy-seven program graduates have attended two-year or four-year colleges or technical schools.

The organization's current needs are to: (1) Expand the program to reach more students, locally and through replication, (2) Dedicate added work hours for new and returning youth, (3) Add additional training support for business, academic, and life skills development modules, and (4) Expand FFTH's distribution, sales, and product line, directly impacting students' financial ability to attend college.

112

Working Against Domestic Violence

National Coalition Against Domestic Violence
P.O. Box 18749
Denver, CO 80218
(303) 839-1852
ncadv.org

Violence begins at home. Children who grow up in violent households become criminals. The National Coalition Against Domestic Violence provides leadership in fighting this domestic terrorism.

Working to stem the tide in domestic violence can be an important contribution to reducing crime against persons and society. The National Coalition Against Domestic Violence is one of the many organizations that can help you get involved.

Violence is the oldest form of domestic terrorism known to humankind. By conservative estimates, four million women in the United States are assaulted by their intimate partner. Approximately 4,000 women die each year at the hands of someone who promised to love them.

In Los Angeles, domestic violence impacts the lives of about 50,000 victims annually. Domestic violence impacts the family, the community and the workplace.

The mission of the National Coalition Against Domestic Violence is to organize for collective power by advancing transformative work, thinking and leadership of communities and individuals working to end the violence in our lives.

NCADV recognizes that the abuses of power in society foster battering by perpetuating conditions which condone violence against women and children. Therefore, it is the mission of NCADV to work for major societal changes necessary to eliminate both personal and societal violence against all women and children.

**Boys & Girls Clubs
of America**
(800) 854-2582
bgca.org

113

Boys & Girls
Clubs Of America

*The mission of the Boys & Girls Clubs of America is to inspire and enable
all young people to realize their full potential as productive, responsible
and caring citizens.*

A Boys & Girls Club provides: a safe place to learn and grow; ongoing relationships with caring, adult professionals; life-enhancing programs and character development experiences; and hope and opportunity.

In every community, boys and girls are left to find their own recreation and companionship in the streets. An increasing number of children are at home with no adult care or supervision. Young people need to know that someone cares about them.

Boys & Girls Clubs offer that and more. Club programs and services promote and enhance the development of boys and girls by instilling a sense of competence, usefulness, belonging and influence. Boys & Girls Clubs are a safe place to learn and grow—all while having fun. They are truly The Positive Place for Kids.

If you want to know more about organizing a Boys & Girls Club, it all begins with wanting to make life better for young people in your community. Once the idea of a Club catches on, you'll find that momentum will build, and you'll be on your way to making a real difference in young lives. The establishment of a Boys & Girls Club usually starts with one or two individuals who initiate the idea and then interest others in the project.

The first step is to discuss your idea of forming a Boys & Girls Club with representatives of service clubs, civic, social, fraternal and labor organizations in your area. They in turn can involve leaders in business, industry and the professions in your community. Network as much as you can in order to stimulate interest in starting a Club—and then do it.

114

YWCA

YWCA of the USA
1015 18th Street NW,
Suite 1100
Washington, DC 20036
(800) YWCA US1
ywca.org

The Young Women's Christian Association has been a pioneer in the empowerment of women and girls since its inception in 1855.

The YWCA of the U.S.A. has been in the forefront of most major movements as a leader in race relations and the empowerment of women and girls, addressing pressing social issues and building coalitions across the lines of class, age, race and ethnicity.

YWCA successes are built by thousands of individuals who donate their time, resources and imagination to create programs, initiatives and an organization tirelessly devoted to women and girls.

The strength of the YWCA movement rests in the spirit and energy of dedicated volunteers who contribute both time and talent to the over 300 YWCAs throughout the Country.

YWCA volunteers engage in all types of activities, including mentoring, membership on the board of directors, fundraising and program assistance.

If you are interested in finding out more about the volunteer opportunities that exist at a YWCA near you, see their website or call.

YMCA of the USA
101 North Wacker Drive
Chicago, IL 60606
(800) 872-9622
ymca.net

115

YMCA

————

Despite its name, the YMCA is not just for the young, not just for men and not just for Christians.

The Young Men's Christian Association is an association of members who come together with a common understanding of the YMCA mission and a common commitment to the YMCA's vision of building strong kids, strong families and strong communities.

Across the United States, 17.9 million members are part of more than 2,400 local YMCA associations. Each association is different, reflecting the needs of the local community. What every YMCA has in common is a dedicated group of people: volunteers, staff, members and donors—all of whom are committed to their mission. Whatever the facilities, whatever the programs, what doesn't change are the people.

Are you interested in having a YMCA in your community? Any community would be enhanced by the presence of a YMCA. Through the experience of starting more than 2,400 YMCAs across the United States, some basic guidelines have been developed to ensure the success of developing new YMCAs in new communities.

A new YMCA typically begins operating programs from donated storefront office space for three to seven years. This provides time and community network building sufficient to start fundraising to build a YMCA facility

If you would like to receive an informational package to help you and other community leaders better understand how to start a new YMCA, contact the YMCA of the USA Network Services.

116

Volunteer
Police Service

*Volunteer Police Service is a program involving seniors and is being
implemented in cities throughout the U.S. with support from the U.S. Citizen
Corps.*

The Retired Senior Volunteer Police program in Huntington Beach, California
recently celebrated its tenth year of operation. Its fifty-six volunteer members
wear special uniforms, drive all-white vehicles and carry out important community safety and protection functions that the regular police may not have time for.

The department estimates that the RSVP group provided services valued at
about $750,000 in savings in officer personnel and time this past year.

Another recent story from Northern California stated that East Palo Alto could
lose more policemen (and women) due to budget cuts, a problem throughout the
Nation. Here is an opportunity for retirees to really help their communities and
enjoy doing it by establishing a volunteer police program.

Many local police departments are turning to civilian volunteers to supplement their sworn force. These vital efforts are receiving new support through the
Volunteers in Police Service Program (VIPS) a program of the U.S. Citizen Corps.
VIPS draws on the time and considerable talents of civilian volunteers and allows
law enforcement professionals to better perform their frontline duties.

You can search the Police Volunteers website for local VIPS programs in your
community and throughout the world. To date, more than 890 law enforcement
volunteer programs, representing more than 61,000 volunteers in all fifty states,
have registered with the VIPS Program.

117

Expanding
Economic Opportunity

The Hope Street Group is an example of a group of business executives who took action to improve the economic status of their community.

The *Los Angeles Times* of June 30, 2003 carried a story "A Vision for Expanding Economic Opportunity." This was about a group of young business executives, most of them based in Los Angeles, who launched an organization dedicated to expanding economic opportunity in their city.

The organization, which they called the Hope Street Group, was founded in 2001 by seven business professionals in their thirties. They developed a series of ideas which they released to the public on their website.

If a group of thirty year-olds can come up with such a program, how about some fifty-five plus year-olds with their seasoned wisdom, experience and contacts?

118

Rubicon

Rubicon Programs Incorporated
2500 Bissell Avenue
Richmond, CA, 94804
(510) 235-1516
rubiconpgms.org

The mission of Rubicon is to help people and communities build assets to achieve greater independence.

Since 1973, Rubicon has built and operated affordable housing and provided employment, job training, mental health, and other supportive services to individuals who have disabilities, are homeless, or are otherwise economically disadvantaged.

Based in Richmond, California, the agency employs upwards of 300 people and offers service throughout Contra Costa County and the San Francisco Bay Area.

Each year, more than 3,000 people participate in one or more of their many programs. Innovative and comprehensive, these programs are designed to meet the diverse needs of the participants, whether they be economic, health-related, or both. Their goal is to provide clients with the tools they need to become self-sufficient and confident in all areas of their lives.

Much of the inspiration for the programs comes from clients themselves, funders, and the community at large. For instance, when participants indicated that housing was a critical need, they found ways to build and operate affordable housing units. Rubicon has developed ten sites in Contra Costa County and two on Treasure Island that offer 180 units. Several of the sites have their own on-site housing counselor and supportive services.

Rubicon has created job training and placement programs. Each year more than 450 people find jobs. Some find jobs within Rubicon Enterprises, a supporting corporation of Rubicon Programs Incorporated. Rubicon Enterprises creates business ventures that train and employ individuals who are entering or re-entering the work force. Its two businesses—Landscape Services and Bakery—employ eighty-one individuals.

Urban Forest Ecosystems Institute Cal Poly State University
ufei.org
Urban Forest Ecosystems Institute University of Georgia
ecology.uga.edu

119

Managing Urban Forests

One way to improve the attractiveness of our communities, and to reverse the trend to asphalt and cement is to develop urban forestry programs in your city.

The *Los Angeles Times* of March 8, 2004 ran an article "No Safe Arbor in the City. " It read in part, "Most people don't realize the significance of the loss, but one man is fighting for a place in the shade. Eric Oldar is a forester and a pioneer in California's tiny urban forestry program, which is tucked away with firefighters in the California Department of Forestry.

"He has devoted most of his twenty-seven year career to promoting urban forests, a concept that makes all the sense in the world, if we think about it. Our cities are turning from green to gray at an alarming rate, and with costly consequences."

An important resource in this battle is the Urban Forest Ecosystems Institute (UFEI) based in the College of Agriculture at California Polytechnic State University, San Luis Obispo, California. It was developed by the Natural Resources Management Department faculty to address the increasing need for improved management of the urban forests in California.

The purpose of the Institute at Cal Poly is to provide a center for: Applied Research; Extension and Technology Transfer; and Community Service and Outreach Programs assisting landowners and public agencies in improving the management of urban forests.

The scope of UFEI ranges across the full spectrum of forest settings—from the inner-city forests to remote semi-developed forests. The Institute is designed to work in co-operation with other universities, government agencies and even private consulting firms.

Another program is active at the University of Georgia.

**International Society
of Arboriculture**
P.O. Box 3129
Champaign, IL 61826
isa-arbor.com

120

International Society
of Arboriculture

*The International Society of Arboriculture is a worldwide professional
organization dedicated to fostering a greater appreciation for trees.*

The International Society of Arboriculture promotes research, technology, and the professional practice of arboriculture. It has served the tree care industry for over seventy years as a scientific and educational organization.

ISA was founded in 1924 when a group of forty individuals, each engaged in a phase of tree work or research, were called together by the Connecticut Tree Protection Examining Board to discuss shade tree problems and their possible solutions. It was during this meeting that the group identified a need for gathering tree care information and for providing a means for its dissemination. The National Shade Tree Conference (NSTC) was founded soon thereafter.

Due to its influence and membership spreading beyond the borders of the United States, the organization changed its name to the International Shade Tree Conference (ISTC) in 1968. Only a few years later, in 1976, in order to more accurately reflect its broadening scope, the name was again changed, this time to the International Society of Arboriculture.

ISA continues to be a dynamic medium through which arborists around the world share their experience and knowledge for the benefit of society. ISA is working hard to foster a better understanding of trees and tree care through research and the education of professionals as well as global efforts to inform tree care consumers.

Today, over sixteen thousand International Society of Arboriculture members invite you to join them in learning what can be done to improve tree care in your community.

Coro National Office
1010 West 39th Street
Kansas City, MO 64111
(816) 931-0751
coro.org

121

Coro Foundation

The Coro Foundation helps groom individuals who are interested in serving their communities by providing programs in public affairs and leadership.

The mission of the Coro Foundation is to strengthen the democratic process by preparing individuals for effective and ethical leadership in the public affairs arena, and thereby strengthen the quality of community and state-wide leadership.

Coro programs immerse participants in the many facets of society to study the intricate relationships among organizations and social systems. Participants experience first-hand the breadth, complexity and pressures of public affairs, developing tools to become leaders.

Coro program participants learn about the real world in the real world by actively questioning, interacting with diverse constituents, finding resources and coming up with innovative solutions to the problems faced by their communities. Together, participants explore community dynamics, leadership and decision-making, while building the skills necessary for successful careers in business, politics, education, government and the nonprofit sectors.

Coro was founded in San Francisco in 1942 when W. Donald Fletcher, an attorney, and Van Duyn Dodge, an investment counselor, launched an exploration of the world of public affairs. Their premise was based on the realization that, unlike law, business or medicine, post graduate training in the area of leadership was non-existent.

As the need for leadership training grew to national proportions, Coro began to explore new territories and established centers in Los Angeles (1957), St. Louis (1972), Kansas City (1975), New York (1980), and Pittsburgh (1999).

Although most centers operate independently with their own board of directors and fundraising, they remain unified in their mission, methods, and goals under the Coro national umbrella. Contact Coro if you have an interest—for yourself or others.

122

Civic Ventures

Civic Ventures
139 Townsend Street,
Suite 505
San Francisco, CA
94107
(415) 430-0141
civicventures.org
experiencecorps.org

Civic Ventures seeks to create compelling opportunities for older Americans to serve their communities.

Civic Ventures also works to promote a richer debate about the roles older men and women can play in the life of this Country, and to generate public policies and other measures enabling older Americans to be more fully involved in strengthening civil society.

Civic Ventures is a national nonprofit organization that works to expand the contributions of older Americans to society, and to help transform the aging of American society into a source of individual and social renewal. Its projects include:

Life Options: To assist adults making a transition from midlife to a new life stage. To capitalize on opportunities to build on their knowledge by providing access to meaningful choices for work, service, lifelong learning and unity connections. These activities play an important role in the health and ongoing development of older adults and provide linkages to the life of the community and its needs.

Experience Corps: A program that engages Americans fifty-five plus in vital public and community service. More than 1,000 Experience Corps members serve as tutors and mentors to children in urban public schools in a dozen cities across the Country. Members help teach children to read and develop the confidence and skills to succeed in school and in life.

Find out how you can participate in these programs, or start a similar program in your community.

Learning, Education

Knowledge is said to double every seven to ten years. To be useful and productive contributors to society, baby boomers and older retirees must continue to stay educated. The more they know about the world around them, the more they can assist others and stay mentally and physically healthy themselves.

A knowledgeable, educated, creative senior is an important resource for society. A disconnected, disinterested, apathetic elder is a liability for society. Our new life expectancies require a redesigned educational format so that lifelong learning is facilitated and rewarded.

Lifelong learning is important to society, but it is more important to the individual. We all want to continue to learn; finding new and interesting ways to do it makes the process that much more enjoyable.

Learning in Retirement has become an important and international activity, with many established venues, as well as the opportunity to create new ones. Several of the established programs and organizations are described in this section.

The ideas presented here provide access not only to learning, but also ways to meet new friends, visit new places and to discover new ways to view older ideas.

University of the
Third Age
harrowu3a.co.uk

123

Universities of
the Third Age

*There are many Learning in Retirement opportunities. Some of these
earlier programs can be helpful in organizing local programs.*

The concept of a place of learning for older and mature citizens with more leisure
time at their hands probably started with the Greeks and Aristotle. It found its
rebirth in France, England and the U.S. beginning about 1962.

The University of the Third Age (U3A) based in the UK aims to encourage men
and women no longer in full-time gainful employment to join together in educational creative/leisure activities.

The program in France began in 1972, followed by the creation of the International Association of U3As (AIUTA). The idea spread throughout the world. The
first British Universities of the Third Age were formed in 1982, under the aegis of
the THIRD AGE TRUST, which became an associate member of AIUTA.

There are now more than 500 local U3A groups throughout the UK, with a
growing membership currently numbering more than 125,000 men and women.
Local U3A groups are autonomous self-help organizations, whose individual
activities are planned and undertaken according to their members' wishes.
Members with a lifetime of experience, expertise or know-how in professions,
occupations or through hobbies are encouraged to form study or activity groups
to share their knowledge with fellow members.

A mutual interest in learning leads to new friendships based on an expanded
social experience. Many study groups meet in members' own homes, adding an
important social dimension.

124

Elderhostel
Institute Network

*The Elderhostel Institute Network (EIN) is a voluntary association of Life
Learning Institutes (LLIs), funded by Elderhostel, Inc., a not-for-profit
organization dedicated to providing educational opportunities for older adults.*

EIN exists to promote communication and provide resources to existing LLIs and to encourage the development of new LLIs. EIN does not prescribe fees or approve curriculum; those decisions are made independently by each LLI. Because LLIs are for local participants, all advertising and registration are handled locally, by each LLI.

The first known Institute for Learning in Retirement (ILR) in the United States was called the Institute for Retired Professionals, created in 1962 in New York City under the sponsorship of the New School for Social Research. During the subsequent twenty-five years, news of the concept spread, primarily by word of mouth and with little media attention.

It was imitated or adapted at other institutions of higher learning, until about fifty such programs existed by 1988. In that year, thirty ILRs collaborated with Elderhostel, Inc. to form a voluntary association known as the Elderhostel Institute Network (EIN). The goals of EIN were to help establish new institutes, provide resources and services to established institutes and develop an all-inclusive organization of institutes for learning in retirement.

Since 1988 the Elderhostel Institute Network has helped start more than 200 new lifelong learning institutes. Today EIN is a resource and communications network for all the programs in North America. EIN also consults on starting new programs and provides help with planning regional LLI conferences.

EIN provides these services to the LLIs through their website which also serves the general public wanting to know more about "learning in retirement."

Omnilore
(310) 540-6011
Redondo Beach, CA
alirow.org/omnilore
ALIROW
alirow.org

125

Omnilore
Association of Learning In
Retirement of The West

Omnilore is a "Learning in Retirement" organization affiliated with California State University at Dominguez Hills.

Omnilore is a group of approximately 220 friendly, fascinating people that is always looking for just a few more souls that like to research and discuss a variety of subjects.

The classes, which meet three times a year in the spring, summer, and fall, have a study-discussion format in which members research topics, give presentations and lead their peers in stimulating discussions (no pressure, no tests, no grades).

They meet for two hours every other week in classrooms in Redondo Beach, CA. The class topics, determined by members, range among philosophy, history, science, literature, drama and art (and everything in-between).

The Omnilore program is associated with Elderhostel and with ALIROW (Association of Learning in Retirement of the West), a group of institutions of higher learning that sponsor LIR programs.

ALIROW can provide information on how to start LIR programs in your area.

North Carolina Center for
Creative Retirement
University of North
  Carolina at Ashville
116 Rhoades Hall
Asheville, NC
  28804-3299
unca.edu/ncccr

126

North Carolina Center
for Creative Retirement

The NCCCR is an activity of the University of North Carolina at Asheville. It has a threefold purpose of promoting lifelong learning, leadership, and community service opportunities for retirement-age individuals.

Most programs are in the Asheville area, but some are carried out in collaboration with other organizations in other parts of North Carolina or across the Country.

NCCCR's long-range goal is to encourage the development of an age-integrated society. In response to the aging of America, NCCCR serves as a laboratory for exploring creative and productive roles for a new generation of retirement-aged people, many of whom will blend education with post-retirement careers.

NCCCR programs and services are guided by a Center Steering Council made up of volunteer leaders who collaborate with the Center's professional staff. The year round programs, which include intergenerational opportunities, serve people in the greater Asheville area. Periodic workshops, seminars and retreats attract individuals from across the Nation.

Their program may serve as a model for similar programs in your part of the Country.

127

Temple University Center for Intergenerational Learning

Temple Center for Intergenerational Learning
1601 North Broad Street, Room 206
Philadelphia, PA 19122
(215) 204-6970
temple.edu/departments/CIL

The Temple University program was created to foster generation to generation cooperation and exchange.

The Center for Intergenerational Learning's programs include:

Experience Corps involving older adult (fifty-five plus) volunteers working in elementary schools to help children succeed by tutoring, reading aloud, storytelling and writing activities. Volunteer as few as two hours a week or as many as fifteen hours a week. Some stipends are available.

Family Friends is an in-home support program in which older adults (fifty-five plus) visit families that have children with disabilities and chronic illnesses. Volunteers visit families once a week for two hours.

Full Circle Theatre is a culturally diverse ensemble of actors, ages fourteen to ninety-two, that uses interactive and improvisational theatre techniques to assist audiences explore social concerns and develop problem-solving strategies. They perform at conferences, schools, hospitals, community and senior centers. They recruit male and female actors (ages fifty-five plus) to participate in the theatre.

Through the development of innovative cross-age programs, the provision of training and technical assistance, and the dissemination of materials, the Center serves as a national resource for intergenerational programming.

**International
Schools Services**
15 Roszel Road
Princeton, NJ 08543
(609) 452-0990
iss.eduiss.edu

128

International
Schools Services

International Schools Services (ISS) is a private, nonprofit organization founded in 1955 to serve American international schools overseas. It seeks educational professionals to help with its worldwide programs.

The Princeton office of ISS is staffed by professionals experienced in the field of international education. ISS also employs teachers and administrators in the schools it operates worldwide.

International Schools Services activities include establishing and operating international schools; recruiting and placing teachers and administrators; consulting; financial management; purchasing and shipping instructional materials, supplies and equipment for schools, colleges, and universities; publishing; foundations management; and facility planning.

The mission of ISS is to advance the quality of education for children in international schools by providing innovative services and solutions for learning communities and corporations throughout the world. This is accomplished by working with all groups that are involved in the education process.

Since 1955, the Educational Staffing services of ISS have successfully assisted over 15,000 qualified teachers and administrators in their search for opportunities in 200 American and international schools around the world. Educators must first apply to establish a professional file with ISS in order to seek an international position through their services.

129

Bringing Entrepreneurism to Our Schools

California Department of Education
1430 N Street
Sacramento, CA 95814
(916) 445-7334
ca.gov

*Getting schools to operate more like businesses
is a goal of many of California's leaders.*

In California, Richard Riordan, lawyer, venture capitalist and former mayor of Los Angeles and state Education Secretary to Governor Arnold Schwarzenegger, is determined to bring entrepreneurial methods to the State's schools. In this effort he has teamed up with William Ouchi, a long-time friend and advisor in this quest to reinvent the State's 8,000 schools.

Ouchi, an author of popular books about teamwork in corporate America, is the behind-the-scenes idea man who argues for turning principals into entrepreneurs, giving campuses new control over their budgets and prodding schools to compete for students. He has written a book, *Making Schools Work*, published in 2003.

These types of efforts have created a great deal of frustration in the past. The Governor, Riordan, Ouchi and others need a lot of help in implementing changes in the system. Ouchi has assembled a group of educators to develop the plan. He has called the think tank IC/3—Independent Citizens for California's Children—and filled the roster with a who's who of education heavyweights.

Find out what you can do to help. You can get similar programs started where you live.

**National Parent
Teachers Association**
1927 Paysphere Circle
Chicago, IL 60674
pta.org

130

Strengthen Our Schools

As retirees, who no longer have to worry about getting our own kids through school, we might think about how we can help the establishment improve our schools, or create new establishments that can be effective.

The Parent Teachers Association, founded in 1897, is the Nation's oldest and largest volunteer education advocacy group. Its current leadership is concerned about the fact that the membership is now about ninety percent white and mostly female.

The organization is competing with an increasing number of independent parent organizations that forego the national hierarchy to focus on local school issues.

Once our kids are out of school, we tend to leave school problems to the current parents. Maybe it is time to think about our grandkids and their kids and do something to help out with your local school district or get involved with the PTA on a national level.

131

National Council on Economic Education

National Council on Economic Education
1140 Avenue of the Americas
New York, NY 10036
(800) 338-1192
ncee.net

One of the institutions focused on improving education is the NCEE, whose programs help students develop economic and personal finance decision-making skills.

The National Council on Economic Education (NCEE) is a nonprofit, non-partisan organization that leads in promoting economic and financial literacy with students and their teachers.

NCEE's mission is to help students develop the real-life skills they need to succeed—to be able to think and choose responsibly as consumers, savers, investors, citizens, members of the workforce, and effective participants in a global economy.

EconomicsAmerica® is NCEE's comprehensive program, which impacts and improves the quality of economic and personal finance education in America's K-12 schools.

Each year, directly and through their affiliated nationwide network of state Councils and over 200 university-based Centers for Economic Education, NCEE's standards-setting materials and resources are used by thousands of teachers to teach millions of students how the "real" world works before they go to work in it.

Contact NCEE to see how you can help increase the impact of their programs or develop your own program in your community.

**Decision Education
Foundation**
745 Emerson Street
Palo Alto, CA 94301
(650) 475-4474
decisioneducation.org

132

Decision
Education Foundation

*The Decision Education Foundation is a nonprofit organization that
works with American youth and educators to improve the effectiveness
of decision-making education.*

The Decision Education Foundation works with large school systems to incorporate decision education into their curriculum in a meaningful way.

DEF relies on a team of exceptional volunteers and a small professional staff to do its work. DEF volunteers are teachers and students, academics and business people, executives and social workers, teenagers and retirees. Many have devoted their professional lives to the study and implementation of good decision practices. All come together in pursuit of an inspiring mission: "Better Decisions—Better Lives."

Both our lives and society are critically shaped by the choices we make as students, professionals, consumers, citizens, and family members. By educating people in decision-making and arming them with effective methods, they are enabled to tackle their choices in a more enlightened and empowered manner. Better decision-making can yield profound benefits for us all. Concentrating initially on American youth through schools, parents, teachers and community organizations, they emphasize projects with immediate benefits and visibility. They pay special attention to youth at greatest risk from poor decision-making.

DEF needs many volunteers to help with curriculum development, teacher training, fundraising, and public relations—this is an opportunity to join a dedicated group of exceptional people inspired by a worthwhile cause.

133

Youth Writing Skills

The ability to write is a critical skill for anyone who wants to be successful in essentially any field. We are well behind in teaching this necessary ability.

"A national test puts California in the bottom third of states," according to an article in the *Los Angeles Times* entitled "Writing Skills Lagging in Grades 4, 8." This report is based on a report from the National Assessment of Educational Progress (NAEP), also known as "the Nation's Report Card."

The NAEP, part of the U.S. Department of Education, is the only nationally representative and continuing assessment of what America's students know and can do in various subject areas. Since 1969, assessments have been conducted periodically in reading, mathematics, science, writing, U.S. history, civics, geography, and the arts.

NAEP does not provide scores for individual students or schools; instead, it offers results regarding subject-matter achievement, instructional experiences, and school environment for populations of students (e.g., fourth-graders) and groups within those populations (e.g., female students, Hispanic students). NAEP results are based on a sample of student populations of interest.

With this information you can see how your state stacks up, not only in writing but the many other areas on which they report. Helping kids in your state or neighborhood can be rewarding, and it is not difficult to get involved. Contact your local schools, or those in areas not as well off as yours, and ask how you can help.

CREATIVE ARTS: MUSIC, WRITING, LITERATURE

*M*any individuals find that retirement is now the perfect opportunity to develop the musical, artistic or literary skills that they wished they had time for earlier. If you find that you don't have the ability yourself, you can learn to appreciate the skills in others.

Studying various aspects of the arts is an excellent way to get more out of the travel experience, by visiting museums, enjoying and appreciating art, monuments and historic sites all over the world, and maybe even writing about those experiences.

Writing about your life is a way to relive your experiences, good and bad, and to leave a legacy to your children and grandchildren. Writing fiction is a wonderful way to find and develop your creative skills. Digging into your heritage, or the heritage of your community and then writing about what you have found is another great way to leave a legacy.

Becoming more proficient in photography or drawing is another way to enhance the travel experience and preserve family memories.

Doing it yourself, studying art in all of its forms, or using the arts to help others are all excellent ways to find fulfillment.

**Art in the Public
Interest/CAN**
P.O. Box 68
Saxapahaw, NC 27340
(336) 376-8404
communityarts.net

134

Community Arts Network
Art in the Public Interest

*Art in the Public Interest has helped establish an organization to provide
information, research and dialogue related to community-based arts
programs.*

The Community Arts Network (CAN) promotes information exchange, research
and critical dialogue within the field of community-based arts; art made as a
voice and a force within a specific community of place, spirit or tradition. CAN
was initiated in 1999 through a partnership between Art in the Public Interest, a
national nonprofit organization, and The Virginia Tech Department of Theatre
Arts' Consortium for the Study of Theatre and Community.

The CAN website provides a portal for news, information, dialogue and networking for people interested in community-based arts. It is edited and maintained by Art in the Public Interest. The website has three primary areas.

APInews: a monthly newsletter reporting items of interest in the field of community-based arts throughout the United States and elsewhere. The newsletter
is also available via email.

CAN Reading Room: a searchable, categorized library of links, articles,
essays and written materials about community-based arts. The Reading Room
features writing commissioned by CAN, writing authored by CAN participants,
writing culled with permission from other sources, and links to useful materials
elsewhere on the web. In addition, the Reading Room serves as an online home
for a number of special research projects such as the "Grassroots Ensemble The-
ater Research Project" and "Connecting Californians."

CAN Conversations: an online forum for anyone interested in sharing information, discussing ideas, and asking questions.

Art in the Public Interest can be a model for other arts supportive organizations throughout the U.S.

135

Elders Share
The Arts

Elders Share the Arts (ESTA) is a New York based community arts organization nationally recognized for its intergenerational work with elders and children.

ESTA recently celebrated its fifteenth anniversary with the publication of *Generating Community: Intergenerational Partnerships Through the Expressive Arts* by Susan Perlstein, ESTA's founding director, in collaboration with Jeff Bliss, the intergenerational arts coordinator.

Generating Community outlines successful models for using the arts in planning and sustaining meaningful connections among generations, and among cultures living in the same communities.

Building on ESTA's Living History work in senior centers, hospitals, nursing homes, schools, colleges and universities, the book is a step-by-step guide to the Living History method pioneered by ESTA in workshops, training sessions, performances and festivals with thousands of older adults, young people and community service professionals—in New York and nationwide.

ESTA intends it as a training manual for use not only in clinical and educational settings, but in libraries, religious organizations, housing projects and youth agencies.

This may be a model for an intergenerational activity for your community.

WriteGirl
Keren Taylor, Executive
Director
(323) 327-2555
writegirl.org

136

WriteGirl

─────

This is the story of how one woman created an activity that provides mentoring help to girls by recruiting successful women to be their partners in developing and strengthening writing skills.

When she lost her job in online sales, Keren Taylor needed a new outlet for her creative energy. She recalled the satisfaction she had gotten as the mentor of a girl when she lived in New York City. That memory inspired her to create an opportunity for girls—especially those at risk of failure or trouble—to escape the pressures of adolescence, discover their artistic voices and just be themselves.

Two months after losing her job, Taylor brought together twenty women and twenty girls for a creative writing workshop. WriteGirl was born. Since then, the nonprofit organization—funded by the Los Angeles Unified School District and the Annenberg Foundation, among other sources—has matched nearly 200 girls with successful women from around the L.A. area who volunteer as one-on-one mentors.

WriteGirl also has monthly workshops during the school year in which all participants write and exchange ideas. The women who run WriteGirl say its relentless concentration on creative writing boosts the girls' confidence and communications skills, while its emphasis on community building and self respect reduces their chances of dropping out of school, abusing drugs, or getting pregnant.

WriteGirl is a model for what might be done in communities all across the U.S. While females are generally perceived as the more sensitive, creative sex, a program oriented for boys could be equally effective.

The idea of keeping the groups single-gender does seem to make sense. The founder of WriteGirl believes a supportive, all female environment is crucial to her philosophy, because "boys do all the talking" when boys and girls mix.

Art & Creativity for Healing
26079 Getty Drive
Laguna Niguel, CA
(949) 367-1902
art4healing.org

137

Art & Creativity
For Healing

Founded in 2000, Art & Creativity for Healing Inc. is a nonprofit organization that facilitates fine arts classes and workshops for children, teens and adults suffering from abuse, illness, grief and stress.

The organization provides free classes and is taught by Founder/Director Laurie Zagon and her team of highly qualified facilitators, on-site at hospitals, treatment facilities and nonprofit agencies throughout Southern California.

They believe that the act of painting can function as a separate language and contribute to the emotional healing process; that the utilization of the creative process through painting can be healing and therapeutic; and that artistic expression of emotions is good for our communities and our culture.

Their objectives are to: introduce the language of expressive feeling through painting; offer free-of-charge workshops and classes where people of all ages and stages can process stress, illness or grief; become a valuable resource for a variety of community organizations in the area of Art & Creativity for Healing; have a positive influence on the community through the use of active outreach programs for underprivileged and at-risk children, teens and their families; mentor and encourage volunteers to give community service through the Art & Creativity for Healing program by interaction with local hospitals, schools and nonprofit community organizations; and train and certify Art for Healing Instructors.

Another model for what can be done in your community.

138

Family History

A site for beginners
jellyjar.org
Mormon Church
familysearch.org
Genealogy Gateway
gengateway.com

Studying and writing about your family history can be fun and rewarding. It is a way for you to understand where you came from and to leave a legacy for your family. Studying the history of your community by studying the genealogy of some of its founders can be the start of a community history project.

Looking into the genealogy of your family, or of other families in whom you have interest, can be enlightening and rewarding. Once you have uncovered the information you can then write the related history.

This can be the history of your family, or a history of your community and the many families that came together to form the initial community. It can be a way of leaving a legacy, for your family and for your community.

The first thing you need to do in getting started searching your family tree is to talk to your family. Ask your parents, grandparents, aunts, uncles, anyone who is willing to share with you. The sooner you start, the more people you will have around to learn from.

Family history can give both interesting clues in genealogy research and thought-provoking tales from the past. Some are amusing or poignant, but never dull. These glimpses into your family history enrich your lives; it is one of the things that makes genealogy rewarding. It is an opportunity to get closer to the members of your family who are still living, and to get to know those who are now history.

Anyone who is interested in getting started doing research on their family's history can find limitless help and information on the Internet. Websites can be found for the new beginning genealogists who need a little help getting started.

Remember to have fun and enjoy yourself. It truly makes history fun by making it more personal to you. Above are some websites to help you get started.

Writers Digest
4700 E. Galbraith Road
Cincinnati, OH 45236
(513) 531-2222
writersdigest.com

The Writer Magazine
Kalmbach Publishing Co.
21027 Crossroads Circle
Waukesha, WI 53187-1612
(262) 796-8776
writermag.com

139

Writing Magazines

There are two major magazines serving writers and aspiring writers, both of which provide how-to, motivational and basic information to help with your writing projects.

Writer's Digest was founded in 1920. Its companion publication, *Writer's Market,* a resource for writers seeking to publish their work, was first published in 1921. These publications form a foundation of a wide range of informational, instructional and inspirational offerings for writers.

The Writer Magazine provides useful up-to-date market news and market listings, advice from top writers like David McCullough, Sue Grafton, and Janet Evanovich, the latest tips from agents and editors, current trends and news from the publishing industry, everything you need to know about copyrights and contracts, and more. Subscribers also gain free access to Web-only articles, hundreds of literary markets and monthly newsletters.

These publications provide a number of offerings for the aspiring writer, including a variety of books, magazines, special interest publications, educational courses, conferences, websites and more. They can help you become the writer you want to be and help you produce the kind of writing editors and agents are looking for.

Discover how to use the Internet to further your writing career, learn the techniques that have helped other writers get published, get the latest market listings, and hear about upcoming conferences and contests.

140

Free-Lance Writing

The Well Fed Writer
Peter Bowerman
3713 Stonewall Circle
Atlanta, GA 30339
(770) 438-7200
wellfedwriter.com

A great way to combine the creative urge to write and make a living at it is free-lance commercial writing, where writing buyers will pay talented and strategically focused writers rates of $50-$125+ an hour for their services.

One resource to get you started on this new, or renewed career, is *The Well Fed Writer*, and its companion, *The Well Fed Writer Back for Seconds* written by Peter Bowerman.

He tells us that the commercial writing field is an excellent opportunity for those nearing or in retirement. You do have to be a reasonably good writer to make decent money in this business, but a background in many businesses will offset some deficiencies.

There are many fields, such as healthcare, banking, manufacturing and technology that have continuing needs for clear, concise copywriting that doesn't have to be a work of art. By studying your junk mail, the little newsletter inserts in your electric bill, the rack brochures at your bank, you can get ideas about companies or publications that can use your help. Your former employer may be a prospective client.

Bowerman's website provides many ideas and resources for the aspiring free-lancer. He has many stories of individuals who have become very successful in turning a hobby into a new, money-making profession.

141

Internet Website Development

One of the easiest ways to exercise your creative writing skills is to develop your own Internet website. It can be on any subject you choose.

Creating your own website is not technically challenging now that there are several services available to help you establish and maintain your presence on the Internet.

The steps are quite simple. Once you decide on your topic and what you would like to accomplish with the site, you need to come up with a unique name for the site. This has to be a name that is not already being used, so you might want to think of several backup alternatives.

You then go to one of the many Internet based services that can determine if your selected name, your URL (Uniform Resource Locator) is available. The process takes about thirty seconds. If it is available, you may reserve it for as short a period as one year, and at a cost under $10.

The service you have selected can then provide help in designing your site and getting it launched on the Internet. The cost can be kept under $200 per year.

It can be very exciting to see yourself in electronic print, and to know that the site can be seen by over 300 million Internet users all over the world. Of course, they have to want to find you.

The process of getting your site connected to eyeballs is the big challenge. You will probably need additional help in the intricacies of attracting the various search engines to your site, including the judicious use of 'metas,' which are words or phrases that search engines will use when a user is looking for information on specific topics.

For Costco customers, they are providing Internet creation and hosting services for $14.95 per month plus a one-time $10 setup fee. To find other help, go to your favorite search engine (Yahoo, Google, MSN, AOL, etc.) and search for something like "internet website services" or "website marketing services," etc. One such service is fortunecity.com.

142

Writing About
Your Travel

Combining travel with writing can enhance the enjoyment of special trips by motivating the individual to do more homework before the trip, to delve more fully into the travel destinations, and by providing a more complete record of the experience. It can also be financially rewarding.

For those interested in writing about their travels, or in researching the travel information business, The Institute for Travel Writing and Photography can be a useful resource to get you started. Each year, the Institute attracts as many retirees as it does new college graduates. The Institute teaches both the business side of travel writing and photography and the creative side.

The Institute is organized to benefit writers, travel writers, photographers and experienced travelers who want to write travel articles or guidebooks or who already do and want to improve their performance in preparing article queries or book proposals, in negotiating contracts, in working with editors, in organizing their time, in self publishing, and in electronic publishing.

The aim of the Institute is to prepare authors to make a good living writing quality articles and guidebooks that serve the traveling public well. The Institute also serves active travelers who want to travel more authoritatively and keep better journals.

The program is provided by the Society of American Travel Writers, which is about fifty years old and has as its purposes the promotion of responsible journalism, professional support, and the encouragement of the conservation and preservation of travel resources worldwide.

Its 1,300 members include writers, photographers, editors, electronic and media journalists, film lecturers, broadcast/video/film producers and public relations representatives.

The Self-Publishing Manual
parapublishing.com
iUniverse, Inc.
iUniverse.com
AuthorHouse
authorhouse.com
Phenix & Phenix
BookPros.com

143

Self Publishing Options

Self publishing used to be looked down on by any respectable author or book reviewer. Now there are so many sources of help that the individual author can create a book every bit as attractive and compelling as those of the leading publishing houses. And keep more of the profits.

If you are contemplating the creation of a book, regardless of topic, finding a publisher can be daunting. First, there are fewer of them due to consolidations in the business. Second, if you are not already established as a writer it is very difficult to even get an agent; and without an agent it is extremely difficult to entice a publisher.

Once you do find a publisher, they take control of your offspring. You lose essentially all control of how the book ends up, and how it is marketed. Finally, your proceeds from sales are going to be around ten percent of the sales price.

Self publishing will cost more up front, since you will have to cover the costs that the publishers normally deal with. However, you retain full control over the production of the book, and retain all of the net proceeds once your expenses are covered. And, the production process will go much more quickly.

Self publishing is becoming more and more accepted. Many popular books have been self published, at least initially. A classic example is *What Color is Your Parachute?*, which has sold millions.

The self publishing firms provide a broad range of tools and services to allow authors to make their own choices throughout the publishing process. Authors typically retain all rights, maintain editorial control and choose the specific services that best suit their goals. The firms can provide a step-by-step process that enable authors to achieve publishing success.

An excellent book to get you started is *The Self-Publishing Manual*, by Dan Poynter.

The address box contains a cross-section of firms offering self publishing assistance and services.

Relationships

If a man does not make new acquaintance as he advances through life, he will soon find himself alone. A man, sir, should keep his friendship in constant repair.
                    ∼ Samuel Johnson

It is vitally important that men and women build and maintain their relationships with others after they retire. Women tend to be better at this than men. Men, and perhaps women who have stayed active in professional or other careers, have most of their important personal relationships through their work. So they have to work harder to create new networks.

When individuals retire, they often lose opportunities for meaningful and fulfilling relationships. If they have not cultivated other types of relationships, or if they are unable to find new sources of relationships, they can quickly become depressed, whether they are willing to admit it or not.

Dr. Andrew Weil, author of the best-selling book *Spontaneous Healing*, in a recent newsletter discusses the value of positive relationships on your health and longevity. He states that there is now a large body of research showing that bonds with family and friends have a powerful influence on not only your emotional well-being, but also your physical health.

The first lines of relationships are with one's family. Those with positive and broad family relationships may not need to seek friends outside that family. However, most individuals, whether they have those family ties or not, will benefit from a broad source of challenging, motivating and fulfilling interaction with others on a continuing basis. The more and better the relationships in your life, the better your health tends to be.

Circle of Men
Bill Kauth
Human Development
Associates, Inc.
4913 N. Newhall Street
Milwaukee, WI 53217

144

Discussion Groups

Forming local, small discussion groups can be an excellent way to develop new, and strengthen older relationships. It is also a way to begin discussing important issues, such as "What are we going to do with the rest of our lives?" Topics can be anything; the more significant, the more lasting the benefits.

The Young Presidents Organization has established "forums" for their members; typically groups of twelve to twenty individuals. These initially gave the company presidents the opportunity to discuss on an intimate and private basis problems or issues in their companies and in their family life.

As individual groups mature, and the CEOs retire, the forums remain as important ways for the individuals to stay close and discuss newer issues related to retirement and aging.

The basis for forming a group can be almost anything. Typically there needs to be some rationale for a group, some local issue or cause. However, once the group is formed, the interaction among the members is the most significant benefit.

The book *A Circle of Men*, by Bill Kauth, is 'the original manual for men's support groups.' It provides information on how to find the right members, running your first several meetings, and what to expect as the group matures.

It is designed to take one through the steps necessary to create an enjoyable, purposeful, and long-lasting group experience. The typical purpose of these groups is to support and help one another in new ways to be—socially, personally, professionally, and in relation to one another. In these groups, individuals can talk about unusually sensitive topics.

Kauth has assisted in the organization of hundreds of such groups. He is the cofounder of The New Warrior Training Adventure, 'one of the oldest and most respected men's initiation organizations' with branches in several cities.

The appendix of the book provides a list of books on the subject of men, masculinity and men's relationships with other men. The application of the ideas in this book is not limited to men.

145

Meetup.com

If you want to start a group on any specific topic, here is an Internet based service that can help you find others and get started.

Meetup.com helps people find others who share their interests or causes, and form lasting, influential, local community groups that regularly meet face-to-face. They believe that the world will be a better place when everyone has access to a people-powered local Meetup Group. That is their goal.

Meetup Groups help people: find the other participants; get involved locally; learn, teach, and share things; make friends and have fun; rise up, stand up, unite, and make a difference; be a part of something bigger—both locally and globally.

Access to the Meetup.com website and use of certain features of their platform is free, at least for now. They do charge fees for various premium features and services that they offer. They also warn that they may change this policy and begin charging for access to their website and other features and services.

They are proud to give more power to the people. They believe it's possible to make a profit and make a difference. Meetup.com earns money from: Meetup Groups that want extra features and services to make them stronger; partner organizations that use Meetup.com services to strengthen their communities; establishments that pay to be listed as a venue that welcomes certain Meetups; and from sponsors who buy text ads relevant to Meetup Group members.

Visit the Meetup.com website to see how it works and how you can get started.

146

Red Hat Society

Women tend to be better at socializing than men. The Red Hat Society is an excellent example of how a small group of women with a fun idea created a worldwide organization. Guys, I know you can do it too!

The Red Hat Society is a fast growing social club open to women fifty and older, founded by Sue Ellen Cooper, of Fullerton, California. In 1997 she gave a red hat (bought at a thrift store) and a copy of the poem "Warning" by Jenny Joseph to a friend in celebration of her fifty-fifth birthday.

The poem begins, "When I am an old woman, I shall wear purple with a red hat which doesn't go, and doesn't suit me." It continues to expound that aging can be fun and freeing. This led to a small group outing and the founding chapter was born in April 1998.

Today there are more than 22,000 chapters across the United States and in twenty-three countries, boasting an estimated 500,000 members. Women get together to have a lot of fun, let their hair down and allow their creativity to come out.

For the members, it is a way to celebrate life after fifty and experience the aging process together. Making new friendships is one of the biggest payoffs of being involved.

To find out about starting a chapter, or for men looking for ideas for creating a male version, visit the Red Hat website.

The Transition
Network
333 West 57th Street,
Suite 8C
New York, NY 10019
(917) 940-5834
thetransitionnetwork.com

147

Transition Network

The Transition Network is a membership organization bringing together women over fifty who have had successful careers and are interested in helping one another in transition.

The Transition Network is a vibrant community of 500 women from the New York City area. Most of the women are in their fifties and sixties, representing a spectrum of professions in business, government, health care, academia, not-for-profits and the arts. Membership is open.

TTN, although currently operating in the New York metropolitan area, is envisioned as a national membership organization intended to involve thousands of women over fifty who have had successful careers and are in or interested in transition.

It is organized as a national network that provides leadership, sets policy, runs a full service website for the organization, supports the development of chapter organizations and provides a voice for the growing population of women over fifty.

It takes the lead on nationwide initiatives such as the organization of symposia on transitions, management of national media coverage to help change the image of retirement, and the development of strategic alliances.

Chapter organizations, under local leadership, will run their own programs by the policies set forth by the national organization. Each chapter will provide a network and a wide range of small group activities for chapter members.

For women, this may be an opportunity to start a new chapter. For men, you might create your own version of TTN.

148

Seniors
Finding Seniors

*One of the important reasons for retirees to get familiar with using the
Internet is the fun they can have looking for a significant other using
the boy-meets-girl resources online.*

Matchmaking via the Internet is becoming very popular and successful. AARP
has added a column to its magazine called "Modern Love" which features tips on
how to use online services and post their own dating stories.

SeniorsMatch promotes itself as "The Only Matching Service Exclusively For
The Over 50 Age Group." They go on to say "Only Love Can Change Your World!
Would you like to meet other singles in your own age group? We have thousands of
other Members in your age group who are seeking personal contact with others. If
you are not a Member of SeniorsMatch How in the World Wide Web will they find
you?"

To use their system, you simply describe yourself and the type of person
you're seeking and their computer will search their database and find compatible
referrals based on your tastes and preferences.

Match.com is another site that has had good experience in matching seniors.
Many others can be found with an Internet search.

149

Seniors
Helping Seniors

*In addition to matchmaking, the Internet can be a great tool for
finding others with similar interests or with special needs.*

Wired Seniors is a portal website designed to serve a wide variety of needs or interests of the over fifty age group. One of its services is to match people with needs for help, or questions, with other seniors who can help them on a specific topic.

It seeks individuals who can provide help to others via the Internet on subjects including home maintenance, gardening, photography, computers, computer software, Internet, cooking, hardware, pets, sports, and trivia.

The site posts various categories and individuals post their questions and others post answers.

They avoid offering help in the areas of finance, health or the law. They suggest individuals consult professionals in those fields.

Find a Need and Fill It

*Do not follow where the path may lead. Go instead where
there is no path and leave a trail.*
　　　　　　　～ Ralph Waldo Emerson

Most of the ideas in the earlier sections of this book are existing
organizations or activities that readers can join and find activities of
interest. The organizations were started by someone who saw a need
or an opportunity and did something about it.

This section introduces, and emphasizes the idea of starting something new; of being the individual who saw a need and took action;
of seeking, finding and asking others to help you.

There are many more needs, and hence opportunities, than an
individual or organization can envision. The more we look, the more
we will find. The more specialized, the narrower the focus, the better
the chance of becoming the guru of that particular problem or need.

Building on a combination of your own interests, experiences, talents, contacts, and exposure to the world's problems and opportunities—and perhaps stimulated and motivated by some of the ideas in
this book—you might consider developing your own special contribution to society.

First, get the idea. Next, find out what is already being done.
Decide what you might try. Seek out some others to help you.
Develop a plan. Do it!

To help get you thinking about things that need fixing, we have presented some problems that could use your help. Your own experiences and imagination can add many others.

Also included are some tools or resources to help you in developing your program. The next step is up to you.

150

Become an Expert

One of the more exotic and potentially rewarding things one can do is to become an expert on something, probably anything.

The amount of knowledge, time and effort required to be smarter than ninety-five percent of the others out there is surprisingly small. The narrower and more esoteric the topic, the less the competition and the smaller the investment of time and study required.

If you are going to be helpful in dealing with any need, the best way to start is to really get to understand it, and its implications.

The Internet makes this project all the more doable. Select a topic. This can be something you have been involved with through your career, a hobby, a chance question, "why, grandpa?", something you saw on TV, or?

Once you have the idea, use Google, Vivisimo, or your other favorite search engine to find out what is available about the topic. Keep following the trails until you have captured all the information on the Web. Talk to the sources mentioned. Start your own primary study. You are on your way.

Now, put up a website, "The Center for the Study of [your topic]", with [you] as Executive Director. Somewhere in the site declare yourself an expert (or the expert) in that field. Stake your claim to being the smartest on the subject. If others disagree, find out why they are smarter and then beat them at their own game.

In this process you may decide that your initial topic isn't all that interesting, but you may find something else (serendipity) that turns you on. You can switch whenever the urge hits you.

Once you are the "Expert," you will be surprised at the great dinner conversations you can have, to say nothing of the possibility of being an expert witness at an exciting trial.

151

Blogging

Blogging was one of the most popular topics during the 2004 presidential election. If you don't know what it is, better learn. If you do know, creating your own just requires imagination, tenacity and a little bit of computer skill.

Web logs, or 'blogs' are essentially online diaries that have been the rage among techies for the past four or five years. They enable people to express political views, make social commentary, or rant and rave about popular topics. At the last count, there were about 2.5 million blogs on the Internet.

A relatively new addition to marketing, Gawker Media, which tracks blogs, reports about ten million blog page views monthly. Some of the bloggers who attempted to receive media credentials to cover the 2004 Democratic Convention were: Hot Flashes from the Campaign Trail, ANWR (the Alaska National Wildlife Refuge), iddybud, the American Street, OxBlog, dinnerforAmerica, INDCjournal, Centerfield, TalkLeft, and electablog.

In a recent article, the *Wall Street Journal* describes a web log by a lawyer who writes about prison sentencing issues (sentencing.typepad.com). The article makes the point that "in the vast reaches of the Internet, blogs are small fry compared to commercial sites such as eBay and Yahoo, but their narrow focus can make them a must-read for the particular community interested in every bit and piece related to the subject at hand."

Blogging can be quite profitable. A *Los Angeles Times* article ("Blogging starts to pay off as advertisers see Web potential," 7/17/04) describes the experience of web log creators who started out with little expectation of financial rewards from their sites. But now they are collecting as much as $3,000 to $5,000 per month by selling ads on their site.

A firm mentioned in the article that specializes in connecting bloggers with advertisers is Blogads. The other sites listed above will help you learn how to set up your own blog.

Chronicle of Philanthropy
1255 Twenty-Third St. NW
Suite 700
Washington, DC 20037
(202) 466-1764
philanthropy.com

152

Chronicle
of Philanthropy

*If you are contemplating the creation of a not-for-profit organization,
the Chronicle of Philanthropy provides broad perspective on what others
are doing and resources to help you get started.*

The Chronicle of Philanthropy is the newspaper of the nonprofit world, with more than 100,000 readers worldwide.

It is the number one news source, in print and online, for charity leaders, fund-raisers, grant makers, and other people involved in the philanthropic enterprise.

Their Philanthropy Careers website offers access to philanthropic opportunities and articles with practical advice on seeking work at nonprofit organizations.

In print, *The Chronicle* is published biweekly. A subscription includes full access to their website and news updates by email. An online-only subscription is also available.

**Glamour Gowns
Project**
(323) 526-6329
Kappa Alpha Theta
kappaalphatheta.org

153

Glamour
Gowns Project

Thanks to the Friends of Child Advocates, the fundraising arm of Court Appointed Special Advocates, teenage girls in foster care in Los Angeles County were able to have stylish dresses to wear to their high school proms this spring.

Members of Kappa Alpha Theta sorority at USC and Occidental College help organize the Glamour Gowns project each year, getting donated and "gently used" dresses and accessories from their more fortunate and affluent sorority sisters and friends.

They then make arrangements for a facility, this time the Brentwood California Presbyterian Church, to house the event. With hundreds of dresses assembled on racks by size, the church's fellowship hall took on the look of a Barney's warehouse sale this past year.

By mid-morning, more than 100 teenagers had shown up at the church. The sorority members helped the "customers," playing the role of fashion advisors.

"I'm so happy," one of the girls said, "now all I need is a date." "I have a couple of options," she added.

This is just an example of what someone with a little imagination and energy can do. Find one group with a need, another with more than they need, and put them together.

For information on the Glamour Gowns project, call the local Los Angeles number, or contact Kappa Alpha Theta sorority.

154

Organize Your
Alumni Group

Creating and/or working with an active organization of individuals with whom you have gone to school or worked throughout your career can be a rewarding experience and an opportunity to work with the group to serve others.

Many companies and other organizations have active alumni groups that stay in touch and share ideas and opportunities. Most colleges and universities maintain such alumni networks, giving those alumni an opportunity to interact throughout the Country and the world.

One example in the professional services field is McKinsey & Company, an international management consulting firm serving the top management of corporations and governments worldwide. It has offices around the world and a prestigious list of alumni and alumnae. The firm maintains active relationships with its alumni and provides an Internet based directory that allows the alumni to stay in touch with one another.

Recently, a number of the McKinsey alums have decided to share their interests in development in emerging economies throughout the world and have formed MAD, McKinsey Alumni in Development. They plan to serve on a pro bono basis to help companies and countries develop and strengthen their economies in a number of ways. Another group of McKinsey alums are focusing their interests in support of nonprofit organizations.

If an organization that you have been associated with has such an alumni organization, why not see how you might get other alums to join you to tackle problems or react to opportunities to help others in meaningful ways? If it does not have an active alumni organization, why not see how you might go about creating one?

155

Kids Without Homes

There must be some way to match the two realities of our times;
there are thousands of huge homes with only one or two residents and
there are thousands of kids with no place to sleep or take a shower.

On March 3, 2004, the *Los Angeles Times* carried a story, "Plight of Kids Without Homes." It stated that "in Los Angeles, there are more than 8,000 children who are homeless every night, living with their families in emergency shelters, transient hotels, sometimes sleeping in their cars, or, if they are lucky, sleeping for a few days at a time on the floors of family or friends."

If we do not take action at all levels and in every sector, homeless families will no longer be "invisible." Think about what you and your friends might do to help out.

156

Less
Fortunate Seniors

*Helping seniors deal with their many problems can be frustrating
but also very satisfying. There but for the grace of God go we.*

An article in the *Wall Street Journal,* April 1, 2003, "A Painful Source of Marital Strife: When an Elderly Parent Moves In" reminds us of the difficulties of aging, not only for the individual but also for their families.

This article points up the problems for families with aging parents who cannot afford, or choose not to use, retirement care facilities. The costs for long-term care are soaring, and the potential rewards of taking in an aged parent are profound. But the damage and related costs to the family can also be devastating.

Perhaps there are ways that other, healthier seniors can be of help.

Sources of help via the Internet, websites that can help locate services or provide support for caregivers to aged relatives or friends, were provided in the article. These can be helpful places to start if this problem is something that strikes a chord.

The family you save may be your own! Check out the above senior agencies and then see if you can help organize a local group.

157

Healthcare Improvement

What can be done to reduce the cost of healthcare without reducing its quality or effectiveness? So far, the big companies, the government, or AARP have not come up with much.

A recent article in the *Wall Street Journal* stated that "thinking about fixing the health-care system can be a real headache." It points out that medical care costs have risen fifty percent in the past ten years. U.S. companies are complaining that they are bearing the brunt of these increases. But what about the unemployed, the retired, the uninsured?

Maybe the answer lies in coming up with some useful compromises. Using generic drugs rather than big name brands is one example. Having your doctor or pharmacist, or someone specializing in medical or pharmaceutical trade-offs discuss your options and what the effects and costs of the various approaches might be is another possibility.

The *WSJ* reported that "Costly drugs extend lives, but confront patients with wrenching choices." Some of these drugs extend lives only a few months or years, or are less toxic. The trade-off of leaving a family with huge medical bills is a consideration for us all.

Getting groups of like-minded individuals together to discuss the problem might be a starting point. Dealing with specific illnesses or health problems is probably easier and more potentially fruitful than taking on the whole healthcare industry.

You may not be able to make a difference, but you might!

158

Medicare
Reform

Beyond the general question of making healthcare less costly is the issue of Medicare and how it can be made more effective.

Does anyone have the solution to the problems with Medicare? A recent *Wall Street Journal* states "Trustees Report Program Is on Track to Go Bankrupt 7 Years Ahead of Projection."

Business Week of 7/26/04 states, "The Congressional Budget Office says that Boomers should fret about Medicare. The gap between promised benefits and dedicated payroll taxes runs into the tens of trillions of dollars. Some judicious means-testing is needed to make Medicare function as a smaller, but real, safety net."

It's difficult for an individual citizen to determine how this problem might be resolved, but it certainly is worth it for all of us to get more familiar with the details. And then to help to conceive and implement smaller steps that could lead to an improvement in the situation, both in terms of financial impact and in quality of healthcare delivered.

A related problem is the large differences that insurers are charging for supplemental Medicare coverage known as Medigap. The *WSJ* recently reported that millions of retirees are paying thousands of dollars more each year than they need to. Helping retirees do the comparison shopping can be a place to start.

Consumers can find more information on the Medicare website.

U.S. Social Security Administration
ssa.gov
Harvard Generations Policy Project
genpolicy.com
Institute for Policy Innovation
ipi.org

159

Fixing Social Security

The problems with our Social Security system have the potential of pitting the younger generations against their parents and grandparents. It is a problem worthy of serious consideration. Do you have any ideas that you would like to put forward?

Our politicians are now getting serious about facing up to the major entitlement deficits that are being exacerbated by the coming baby boomer tidal wave. When Social Security was introduced in 1935, there were forty contributors to the system for each retiree. Today that ratio is three to one, and getting worse. The life expectancy in 1935 was sixty-three; today it is eighty.

Various approaches have been discussed. Simply stated, there will have to be some combination of tax increases for the young, increases in government borrowing, or cuts in benefits for the elderly. More specific ideas include lowering cost of living increases, raising the full retirement age, increasing the Social Security tax rate and the maximum amount of income that is taxed, and reducing benefits for the wealthiest elderly.

Another plan is to allow individual wage earners to place a percentage of their Social Security contributions into personal accounts which they would be able to monitor and direct in a select group of investments.

As a minimum, taxpayers of all ages should become better informed about the system, its problems, and the merits and problems associated with any proposed "fix." There are two recent books on the subject: *The Coming Generational Storm*, by Kotlikoff and Burns; and *Running on Empty*, by Petersen.

The more ambitious of you might want to become involved in local or state-wide groups to focus on the problems, to evaluate proposed solutions and to help get the best solutions enacted. An important aspect of this problem is that of getting the various age groups to share the pain equally.

The websites above can give you some basic information to begin your quest for solutions.

160

Prison
System Reform

*Most of us have not had the experience of being in prison, or of having
to get readapted to society once we get out. Become more sensitive
to the problems of the penal system, and how prisoners can learn
and improve their lives with the experience.*

California's new governor, Arnold Schwarzenegger has been besieged by reports
of corruption and mismanagement within the State's prisons. In February 2004
he named a woman, Jeanne Woodford, as new head of the State's Department
of Corrections. She had been the warden at San Quentin.

This could open an opportunity for caring, knowledgeable, creative seniors to
become more involved with the corrections process in California, and for others
in the other states to take a similar interest.

The opportunities to have a positive impact on our society could not be
greater.

161

Reducing
Fiscal Waste

We all know that we spend much more on solving problems through government programs than if we managed that money ourselves. How can we get active in reducing the waste and still maintain important programs?

The *Los Angeles Times* of March 23, 2004 stated, "Sacramento Finds Small Savings Count Now."

They have always counted. But it is only when there are problems measured in the billions of dollars do politicians seem to become concerned.

How about getting back to "a penny saved is a penny earned?" The larger a community or society becomes, the more distant the individual taxpayer is from the decisions that affect his or her pocketbook. There are any number of ways that this distance can be shortened; to bring more fiscal responsibility back to the individual. Let's see if we can come up with some ideas, and then get them implemented.

162

World Poverty

How can you, as an individual, do something about world poverty?

Probably not much, but a group of you might do something, and a larger organization that you might start could do a lot more. Think about it.

An article in the *Wall Street Journal* of July 9, 2003 states: "If We Cared To, We Could Defeat World Poverty." It stated, "The great paradox of our time is that the massive suffering of the world's poor—from disease, hunger, unsafe water and more—could be readily overcome by just a modicum of help from the richest countries."

What an individual can do to help alleviate this problem is hard to determine. But wouldn't it be interesting to explore?

obesity.org/subs/childhood
pediatriconcall.com/
 forpatients/commonchild/
 obesity
*Food Fight: The Inside Story of
the Food Industry, America's
Obesity Crises & What We Can
Do About It,* Kelly D. Brownell,
Ph.D.

163

Childhood
Obesity

*Two-thirds of American adults are seriously overweight or obese.
The place to begin winning this battle is with our children.*

An article in *Parents Magazine* of September 2003 is entitled, "The Big Issue—Childhood obesity is quickly becoming an epidemic." The number of overweight children is three times higher today than it was twenty-five years ago. More than fifteen percent of school-age kids are too heavy; weight related childhood diabetes has skyrocketed; and the risk of other health problems continues to climb.

The State of California has estimated the cost of inactivity, overweight and obesity at $24.6 billion a year in private and public medical services, lost productivity and workers compensation in the State. U.S. taxpayers spent $75 billion in Medicaid and Medicare funds treating obesity-related illnesses in 2003.

A study from Rand Corporation predicted that within the next twenty years obesity-linked disease in the U.S. will cancel out health strides caused by improvements in medical technology and disease-fighting measures such as vaccinations.

Teaching our children at a very young age the dangers of smoking has had results. We need to apply more of these early year programs for children to the subject of positive nutrition and its impact on their lives.

Parents need help, the school systems need help, the kids need help, and the food industry needs incentives to do better. What can you do about this problem? As a grandparent or other non-parental relative or friend, it is difficult to deal directly with an at-risk child. But there are ways to get behind and support programs dealing with the problem—or develop your own ideas.

Someone is going to come up with some very effective new ideas to help alleviate this problem. It could be you.

164

Corporate Governance
Investor Activism

*We have all been appalled at the ways that many of the boards of directors
and top executives of our largest, most respected companies have violated
their investors' trust, with corrupt business practices, obscene compensation
and other immoral and illegal acts.*

We can't leave it up to the big guys and government agencies. The individual
investor must become more involved in corporate governance by showing their
interest and attention.

The squeaky wheel does get attention. If corporate directors know that shareholders are watching them, they will be much more careful and attentive when
they vote on issues affecting the longer term outlook for the companies they are
responsible for.

Do your homework, attend shareholder meetings, ask questions, get close to
the corporate officers, make noise.

One place to start with this activity is the Security and Exchange Commission's website.

165

Help Others Find Their Passion

*This book is about finding something that you can get passionate about,
that will be fulfilling and meaningful to you, that will be some kind of legacy
for your children and grandchildren. Perhaps there are ways you can
help others find their passion.*

Get together with your friends and neighbors, other family members. Find out what their concerns and interests are. Discover some common interests and build from there.

Use some of the ideas in this book to start the conversation. See if you can't help your friends create something that will give them a reason to get up in the morning; something that they will be proud to talk about and to get others involved in.

Once you have come up with your vision, or helped others find theirs, share it with us. There are millions of ideas—we just need to put them into action.

Taking Action

Everyone who asks, receives; the one who seeks, finds; and to the one who knocks, the door will be opened
~ Matthew 7:7

Once you have made a decision, even a preliminary "maybe I will and maybe I won't," you will want to do something about it. Contact the organization or do your own research, learn more about the idea or need, plan your next steps, and take action.

The key is to take that next step, and then the next and the next.

Learning More

The first step, once you see something that looks interesting, is to contact the sponsoring organization, if there is one. The website is probably the place to start. Most of the organizations have well established sites, with enough information to tell you what they do, who they are (see the 'About Us' section of the site), their mission, and some examples of what they are doing.

To learn more about the organization, and to get more perspective on its activities and how it is viewed by others, do a search, using Google or one of the other search engines, using the organization's name. Getting experience in using the various search engines will be invaluable. So do some searches just to get good at it. These searches, both on the Internet and at your local library, should give you leads to news items and articles that may have been written about the organizations and their principals, and any news about them and the need they are addressing.

Next, you can go to the 'Contact Us' part of the Internet website and send an email, asking any questions you may have. One of these questions would be whether they are active in your area, or where the closest activity is.

You should find out who sponsors or funds their activities. Who is really behind the organization? Ask for more information on how the activity evolved. What is required of individuals who are interested in participating? What fees or expenses might be involved? What are they selling?

As a next step, or as a replacement for the email contact, call the organization and speak to the person in charge. Learn what they are doing currently, and what opportunities there might be for you. Get some names and contact information for people who are active with the organization in your area.

An Action Plan

Once you have decided that this is something in which you have an interest, take the time to lay out a plan and projection of what you might do if you did get involved. How does it relate to your interests and goals? If you do get involved, how much time will you have to commit? How might it interfere with your other activities?

How would this activity compare to those other things you are doing, in terms of the activity itself. How fulfilling might it be? Is this something you would like to talk about with your friends and family?

One of the approaches that I like to take whenever I think about going into a new venture, or adventure, is to treat it like starting a new business. A book that I often use as a basic business planning text is *Entrepreneuring—the 10 Commandments for Building a Growth Company*, by Steven C. Brandt. It was first published in 1983 and it is still popular. It discusses a number of things to consider before you go into the venture, such as: who will you be associating with, what business or activity will you really be in, the need to make a serious commitment, and walking before you run.

The section on preparing a business plan includes answering:

- What is the basic concept of the venture?
- What are the objectives of the venture and your objectives in being involved?
- What is the market or constituency you will be serving?
- What will be involved in producing the product or service you may be asked to provide?
- Who will you need to work with?
- What are the financial implications? and
- What can you realistically accomplish?

Another, newer book is *The Art of the Start*, by Guy Kawasaki, a Palo Alto-based venture capitalist. It is particularly helpful if you are going to want to raise some capital to move your vision along.

Next Steps

Once you have gone through a process of reflection and planning, what is your next step? What do you do to get started? How do you maintain your enthusiasm and not take the easy way out. A book that is good at motivating you to take action is *Do It! Let's Get Off Our Buts,* by John-Roger and Peter McWilliams. They refer to their book as 'a guide to living your dreams.'

The authors make the point that we often identify something we would like to do, to pursue our 'heart's desire' but we use the time and talent required to do something else—something that keeps us from pursuing that heart's desire. The book helps keep us focused on what it is we really want to do, to move out of our 'comfort zone' and to pursue our dream.

An important element in all of this planning is deciding who you would like to include in the venture. We all need a support system. Who will you want to involve? Your family, close friends, business or professional associates may have some complementary talents to help you be successful. There is probably someone who is particularly talented, experienced or connected.

One of my ideas has been the development of a financial services organization focused on helping seniors better utilize the financial assets tied up in their homes. The 'reverse mortgage' concept is a good one, but it has many limitations, including the amount of money you can actually obtain, compared to the value of the home. So I have approached many of my banker friends to get their opinions and ideas to help make the idea a reality. Even if nothing comes of it, I have reestablished some old relationships and made several new ones.

Side Benefits

The last comment points up one of the important reasons for getting serious about one or more of the ideas that have been presented here, or developing your own ideas. It's the relationships that the associated activities allow you to develop.

There are the direct relationships that come from asking others to help you pursue the selected idea. There are also the relationships with the other people you meet and get to know, just by asking them for their help, or answering their question "So what are you doing these days?"

It's A Wrap!

I hope you will find as much fulfillment in your quest as I have. Once I decided to see if I could help others find a worthy purpose in their retirement, it opened a whole new world to me. I first had to understand what the retirement community was all about—who it was, how many there are, what they are doing and not doing, who is helping them.

Then as I decided to create this guidebook I had to identify worthy ideas to suggest, organize my thoughts, and get them down on paper. Next, I had to learn the publishing business so that I could provide help to those who were producing the book, and to those who were helping to market it.

Now I am looking at ways to use the book as a base for other activities that can help make retirement a productive, useful period in everyone's life. I could not be more happy or fulfilled! I have certainly been enriched.

☙

So, make a list of the things you are going to have to do, put some specific dates against that list, and get on with it!

Give Us Feedback

Our plan is to update this guidebook periodically. We would like to ask all of our readers to forward to us any comments on the ideas presented here. What were your experiences as you attempted to find out more about the activity? Had the organization changed in significant ways? How could the information be presented more usefully or accurately?

Are there any other activities you have been involved in, or that you have become aware of that we should consider for future editions? Do you have any other ideas for such activities? Real life examples of what has been accomplished are of particular interest.

We also welcome any general comments and suggestions for improvement. Please forward them to BruceJuell@CreativeSeniors.com.

God bless!

Appendices

APPENDIX A

Activity Ideas — Alphabetical With Websites

1-800Volunteer	1800Volunteer.org
AARP	aarp.org
Alternative Spiritual Paths	
Buddhism	buddhism.about.com
Yoga	yogabasics.com
Sufism	sufism.org
Wicca	wicca.org
American Red Cross	redcross.volunteermatch.org.
American Youth Hostel	hiayh.org
America's Promise	americaspromise.org
America's Second Harvest	secondharvest.org
American Society of Volunteer Services	asdvs.org
Art and Creativity for Healing	art4healing.org
Backpacking for Seniors	
Lonely Planet Publications	lonelyplanet.com
Federation of International Youth Travel Organizations	fiyto.org
Become An Expert	google.com
Beyond Shelter, Inc.	beyondshelter.org
Big Brothers Big Sisters of America	bbbsa.org
BizBuySell	bizbuysell.com

Discussion Groups
Earthwatch Institute   earthwatch.org
Elderhostel   elderhostel.org
Elderhostel Institute Network   elderhostel.org/ein/intro.asp
Elders Share the Arts   communityarts.net/readingroom/
                                        archive/esta68.php
Entrepreneur Magazine—   entrepreneur.com/franzone
    Franchise Zone
Entrepreneurs Source   theesource.com
Environmental Alliance for   easi.org
    Senior Involvement
Expanding Economic Opportunity   hopestreetgroup.com
Executive Director, Not For Profit filmaidinternational.org
Executive Service Corps   escus.org
Expense Reduction Analysts   erausa.net
Experience Works   experienceworks.org

Family History
    Genealogy Gateway   gengateway.com
    Jelly Jar   jellyjar.org
    Mormon Church   familysearch.org
Fighting High Drug Costs   theseniorinitiative.org
Find Grant Opportunities   grants.gov
Fire Corps   firecorps.org
Follow VC Investment Activities   venturewire.com
Food From the Hood   foodfromthehood.com
Foundation for Teaching Economics   fte.org
Freelance Writing   wellfedwriter.com
Fulfillment Fund   fulfillment.org

Global Crossroad   globalcrossroad.com
Glamour Gowns Project   kappaalphatheta.com
Global Volunteers   globalvolunteers.org
Goddard School   goddardschool.com

Habitat for Humanity   habitat.org
Halftime   halftime.org

Healthcare Improvement

Healthcare Opportunities Begin   google.com
    at Home

Hospitality Club   hospitalityclub.org

Hospital Volunteers   asdvs.org

Hostelling International USA   hiayh.org

Idea List   idealist.org

Intelligent Office   intelligentoffice.com

Interaction   interaction.org

International Executive Service   iesc.org
    Corps

International Fund for Animal   ifaw.org
    Welfare

International Home Exchange   ihen.com

International Rescue Committee   theirc.org

International Schools Services   iss.edu

International Society of   isa-arbor.com
    Arboriculture

International Volunteer   volunteerinternational.org
    Programs Association

Internet Website Development   fortunecity.com

Job Hunting on the Internet

    Career Builder   careerbuilder.com

    Head Hunter   headhunter.net

    Hot Jobs   hotjobs.com

    Monster   monster.com

Kids Without Homes

Less Fortunate Seniors   eldercare.gov

L.A. Biomedical Institute   labiomed.org

Lower Cost Medication Help   helpofojai.org

Managing Urban Forests   ufei.org

Medicare Reform   medicare.gov

MentorNet   mentornet.net

National Council on Economic Education	ncee.net
National Geographic Expeditions	nationalgeographic.com/ ngexpeditions
National Institutes of Health	nih.gov
National Mentoring Center	nwrel.org/mentoring
National Mentoring Partnership	mentoring.org
National Retiree Volunteer Coalition	nrvc.org
Neighborhood Transformation	pointsoflight.org/programs/ neighboring
Neighborhood Watch	citizencorps.gov/programs/watch
NetHope	nethope.org
New Directions	newdirections.com
New Venture Investment	
Tech Coast Venture Network	tcvn.org
Southern California Investment Association	sciaonline.org
California Capital Marketplace	ccmarketplace.org
North Carolina Center for Creative Retirement	unca.edu/ncccr
Omnilore Learning in Retirement	alirow.org/omnilore
Online Travel Guidebooks	www.turkeytravelplanner.com
Outward Bound	outwardbound.org
Over the Hill Gang	othgi.com
Park Cities Presbyterian Church	pcpc.org
Peace Corps	peacecorps.gov
Pharmacy Maven	aphanet.org
Points of Light Foundation	pointsoflight.org
Princeton Project 55	project55.org
Prison System Reform	
Rebuilding Together	rebuildingtogether.com

Red Hat Society	redhatsociety.com
Reducing Fiscal Waste	
Renew International	renewintl.org
Researching Medical Options	thehealthresource.com
Rubicon	rubiconpgms.org
Retired and Senior Volunteer Program	seniorcorps.org
Saddleback Church	saddleback.com
Samaritan House Clinic	samaritanhouse.com
SCORE	score.org
Self Publishing	
AuthorHouse	authorhouse.com
iUniverse, Inc.	iuniverse.com
Parapublishing	parapublishing.com
Phenix & Phenix	bookpros.com
Senior Initiative	theseniorinitiative.org
Senior Job Bank	seniorjobbank.org
Seniors Finding Seniors	seniorsmatch.com
Seniors Helping Seniors	wiredseniors.com/helpingseniors
Seniors Vacation & Home Exchange	seniorshomeexchange.com
Shelter Partnership, Inc.	shelterpartnership.org
Social Entrepreneuring	ventures.yale.edu/default.asp
Social Networking	
CareerChangeNetwork.com	careerchangenetwork.com
Friendster	friendster.com
Linked In	linkedin.com
Zero Degrees	zerodegrees.com
Social Security	ssa.gov
South Central Scholarship Fund	trishahen@earthlink.net
Spiritual Eldering Institute	spiritualeldering.org
Spirituality.com	spirituality.com
Stand Up for Kids	standupforkids.org
StartupJournal	startupjournal.com
Strengthen Our Schools	pta.org

Temple Center for Intergenerational Learning	temple.edu/departments/cil
Transition Network	thetransitionnetwork.com
Trees vs. Cement	ecology.uga.edu
U.S. Coast Guard Auxiliary	cgaux.org
Universities of the Third Age	harrowu3a.co.uk
Volunteer America	volunteeramerica.net
VolunteerMatch	volunteermatch.org
Volunteer Police Service	policevolunteers.org
Volunteers in Medicine	hiltonheadisland.com/vim
Volunteers for Prosperity	volunteersforprosperity.gov
Volunteers of America	voa.org
Walking Works	walkingworks.com
Wildlife Conservation Society	wcs.org
Willow Creek Association	willowcreek.org
World Poverty	
World Vision	worldvision.org
Working Against Domestic Violence	ncadv.org
Writegirl	writegirl.org
Writers Digest	writersdigest.com
Writer Magazine	writermag.com
Writing about Travel	infoexchange.com
YMCA	ymca.net
Youth Writing Skills	nces.ed.gov/nationsreportcard
YWCA	ywca.org

Seniors/Retirees Websites

50something.com	A community of active, computer-using adults, around age 50 on up
aahsa.org	The American Association of Homes and Services for the Aging
ageworks.com	The latest information on aging developed by the faculty of the Leonard Davis School of Gerontology at the University of Southern California
aghe.org	Association for Gerontology in Higher Education
agingresearch.org	Alliance for Aging Research
agingstats.gov	Federal Interagency Forum on Aging-Related Statistics. The U.S. government site for all government programs available on the Internet
asaging.org	American Society on Aging
agingtoday.org	American Society on Aging's bimonthly newsletter
aoa.gov	Administration on Aging
crea.berkeley.edu	Center for Research and Education in Aging at the University of California
firstgov.gov	U.S. Government's official web portal for all types of government services and contacts with Federal agencies
geron.org	Gerontological Society of America
grandtimes.com	Grandtimes seniors portal

ilcusa.org	International Longevity Center-USA
longevitymeme.org	Longevity Meme is a California based organization founded to encourage achievable technologies and other means to help people live comfortably, healthily and capably for as long as they desire.
ncoa.org	National Council on Aging
networkforgood.org	An Internet volunteer and charitable resource sponsored by many leading companies; individuals can donate, volunteer and get involved with issues they care about
seniorlivingnewspaper.com	A portal for a wide range of services of interest to retirees and seniors
seniorssearch.com	A portal to serve the needs of the over 50 age group

Bibliography

AARP, *Think of Your Future*, HarperCollins, 1995

Laurence G. Boldt, *How to Be, Do, or Have Anything*, Ten Speed Press, 2001

Richard N. Bolles, *What Color Is Your Parachute?*, Ten Speed Press, 2004

Richard N. Bolles, *The Three Boxes of Life,* Ten Speed Press, 1981

Walter M. Bortz II, *Dare to be 100,* Fireside, 1996

Steven C. Brandt, *Entrepreneuring*, Archipelago Publishing, 1997

Bob Buford, *Halftime*, Zondervan, 1994

Jimmy Carter, *The Virtues of Aging*, Random House

Deepak Chopra, *Ageless Body, Timeless Mind,* Three Rivers Press, 1993

Gene Cohen, *The Creative Age,* Avon Books, 2000

Mihaly Csikszentimihaly, *Flow*, Harper Perennial, 1990

Ken Dychtwald, *Age Wave,* Bantam Books, 1990

Ken Dychtwald, *Age Power,* Putman, 1999

Erik Erikson, Joan Erikson, Helen Kivnick, *Vital Involvement in Old Age,* W.W. Norton, 1986

Marc Freedman, *PrimeTime*, Public Affairs, 1999

Betty Friedan, *The Fountain of Age*, Simon & Schuster, 1993

Connie Goldman and Richard Mahler, *Secrets of Becoming a Late Bloomer,* Stillpoint Publishing, 1995

Bill Kauth, *A Circle of Men,* St. Martin's Press, 1992

Harold Koenig, *Purpose and Power in Retirement,* Templeton Foundation Press, 2002

Laurence Kotlikoff, *The Coming Generational Storm,* MIT Press, 2004

Jim Miller, *The Savvy Senior,* Hyperion, 2004

Thomas Perls, Margery Hutter Silver, *Living to 100,* Basic Books, 1999

Robert D. Putnam, *Bowling Alone,* Simon & Schuster, 2000

Richard M. Restak, *Older & Wiser,* Simon & Schuster, 1997

Phil Rich, Dorothy Sampson, Dale Fetherling, *The Healing Journey Through Retirement,* John Wiley & Sons, 2000

John-Roger and Peter McWilliams, *Do-It!,* Prelude Press, 1991

Alan Rowe, *Creative Intelligence,* Prentice Hall, 2004

Joel Savishinsky, *Breaking the Watch,* Cornell University Press, 2000

Zalman Schachter-Shalomi, *From Age-ing to Sage-ing,* Warner Books, 1997

Nancy K. Schlossberg, *Retire Smart Retire Happy,* American Psychological Association, 2004

Edward Schneider, *AgeLess,* Rodale, 2003

Barbara Sher, *I Could Do Anything—If Only I Knew What it Was,* Delacorte Press, 1994

Peter Silton, *Active Retirement for Affluent Workaholics,* NP Financial Systems, 2001

Mary Helen Smith and Shuford Smith, *The Retirement Sourcebook,* Lowell House, 1999

Marika and Howard Stone, *Too Young to Retire,* Plume, 2004

Robert L. Veninga, *Your Renaissance Years,* Little, Brown and Company, 1991

Patricia Wagner, Barbara Day, *How to Enjoy Your Retirement—Activities from A to Z,* VanderWyk & Burnham, 2002

Andrew Weil, *Spontaneous Healing,* Random House, 1995

Andrew Weil, *Dr. Andrew Weil's Self Healing* newsletter

APPENDIX D

Government Programs

Federal Seniors Programs

The most highly organized and best funded programs for seniors or retirees are those available through the U.S. Government. These are also the most costly to the U.S. taxpayer. The following is a brief overview of these programs.

- **Older Americans Act (aoa.gov)**

The Older Americans Act was originally signed into law by Lyndon Johnson in 1965, with funding of $5 million. In 1988 it was funded at the level of $1 billion, and it was substantially amended in 2000, adding even more programs and cost. That amendment extended the life of the Act to 2005. The following is a brief overview of the currently available programs covered by the Act.

- **USA Freedom Corps (usafreedomcorps.gov)**

Most of the Federal volunteer programs fall under the USA Freedom Corps, a coordinating council housed at the White House and chaired by the President. President Bush created the USA Freedom Corps to coordinate citizen volunteer efforts both domestically and abroad; to work to strengthen the culture of service and help find opportunities for every American to start volunteering. As part of that initiative, the President called on all Americans to devote the equivalent of at least two years of their lives, 4,000 hours to service and volunteerism. National and community service programs are one way to answer the President's call.

National Service Programs

• Americorps (americorps.org)

Created in 1993, AmeriCorps is a network of national service programs that engage more than 50,000 Americans each year in intensive service to meet critical needs in education, public safety, health, and the environment. AmeriCorps members serve through more than 2,100 nonprofits, public agencies, and faith-based organizations. They tutor and mentor youth, build affordable housing, teach computer skills, clean parks and streams, run after-school programs, and help communities respond to disasters.

President Bush has asked AmeriCorps to expand its work in public safety, public health, and disaster relief to assist in homeland security. The President has also proposed expanding AmeriCorps as part of his USA Freedom Corps initiative. AmeriCorps is made up of three programs: AmeriCorps State and National, AmeriCorps VISTA, and AmeriCorps NCCC (National Civilian Community Corps).

*AmeriCorps*State and National.* More than three-quarters of AmeriCorps grant funding goes to Governor-appointed State Commissions, which in turn distribute and monitor grants to local nonprofits and agencies. The other quarter goes to national nonprofits that operate in more than one state.

The organizations receiving grants are responsible for recruiting, selecting, and supervising AmeriCorps members. AmeriCorps grantees include national groups like Habitat for Humanity, the American Red Cross, and Boys and Girls Clubs, as well as many small faith-based and community organizations. Approximately 44,000 members served in AmeriCorps State and National programs in fiscal year 2001.

*AmeriCorps*VISTA.* For more than thirty-five years, AmeriCorps*VISTA members have been helping bring individuals and communities out of poverty. In fiscal 2001, approximately 6,000 AmeriCorps VISTA members served in 1,200 local programs. Members serve full-time for a year in nonprofits, public agencies and faith based groups throughout the Country, working to fight illiteracy, improve health services, create businesses, increase housing opportunities, or bridge the digital divide.

AmeriCorps*NCCC (National Civilian Community Corps). AmeriCorps*NCCC is a ten-month, full-time residential program for men and women between the ages of eighteen and twenty-four. AmeriCorps*NCCC combines the best practices of civilian service with the best aspects of military service, including leadership and team building. Members serve in teams of ten to fifteen members. Priority is given to projects in public safety, public health, and disaster relief. Teams are based at one of five campuses across the Country but are sent to work on short-term projects in neighboring states.

• Citizen Corps (citizencorps.gov)

Citizen Corps is a vital component of USA Freedom Corps. It was created to help coordinate volunteer activities that will make our communities safer, stronger, and better prepared to respond to any emergency situation. It provides opportunities for people to participate in a range of measures to make their families, their homes, and their communities safer from the threats of crime, terrorism, and disasters of all kinds.

Citizen Corps programs build on the successful efforts that are in place in many communities around the Country to prevent crime and respond to emergencies. Programs that started through local innovation are the foundation for Citizen Corps and this national approach to citizen participation in community safety. Citizen Corps is coordinated nationally by the Federal Emergency Management Agency. In this capacity, FEMA works closely with other Federal entities, state and local governments, first responders and emergency managers, the volunteer community, and the White House Office of the USA Freedom Corps.

Citizen Corps programs include Neighborhood Watch, Volunteers in Police Service, Medical Reserve Corps, and Citizen Corps Councils.

- ### Learn and Serve America (www.learnandserve.org)

Learn and Serve America links classroom studies with service in the community. It is an important and effective way of instilling the habits of good citizenship and fostering a lifelong ethic of service among young Americans.

Learn and Serve America supports service-learning programs in schools and community organizations that help nearly one million students from kindergarten through college meet community needs, while improving their academic skills and learning the habits of good citizenship. Its grants are used to create new programs or replicate existing programs, as well as to provide training and development to staff, faculty, and volunteers.

- ### Peace Corps (peacecorps.org)

Peace Corps is one of our selected ideas and is covered in the Peace Corps page.

- ### Senior Corps (seniorcorps.org)

Senior Corps taps the skills, talents, and experience of older Americans to help solve pressing social problems. It has a thirty-year history of leadership in senior volunteer service and engages nearly a half a million Americans age fifty-five and older in service efforts across all fifty states. There are more than 1,200 Senior Corps programs operating in communities throughout the U.S. through a national network of three projects: Foster Grandparent Program, Senior Companion Program, and the Retired and Senior Volunteer Program (RSVP).

Foster Grandparent Program. Foster Grandparents serve as mentors, tutors, and caregivers for at-risk children and youth with special needs through a variety of community organizations, including schools, hospitals, drug treatment facilities, correctional institutions, and Head Start and day-care centers. In fiscal year 2001 more than 30,000 Foster Grandparents tended to the needs of 275,000 young children and teenagers. Local nonprofit organizations and public agencies receive grants to sponsor and operate local Foster Grandparent projects.

Senior Companion Program. Open to healthy individuals age sixty and over with limited incomes. All applicants undergo a background check and a telephone interview, as well as pre-service and in-service training on such topics as Alzheimer's disease, diabetes, and issues related to mental health. Senior Companions serve twenty hours a week.

Retired and Senior Volunteer Program (RSVP). RSVP is one of our selected ideas for creative senior involvement and is covered in that section.

Volunteer Service Initiatives

• Volunteers for Prosperity (volunteersforprosperity.gov)

Volunteers for Prosperity is one of our selected ideas for creative senior involvement and is covered in that section.

• American History, Civics and Service

On September 17, 2002, President George W. Bush observed the 215th anniversary of the signing of the United States Constitution by announcing new policies and initiatives to support the teaching of American History and Civics and provide Americans with greater access to some of our Country's national treasures.

• Students in Service to America (studentsinservicetoamerica.org)

More than 130,000 public and private elementary and secondary schools, home schools, and after-school programs around the Country have received copies of the Students in Service to America guidebook, a CD-ROM, posters and other teaching and community resources.

• Take Pride in America (takepride.gov)

Take Pride in America engages individuals nationwide in efforts to preserve and protect our natural resources and open spaces, generating more than twelve million hours among individuals and groups in volunteer service.

More information about the various Federal volunteer programs, and how to participate in any of them, can be obtained at: The Corporation for National Service, 1201 New York Avenue NW, Washington, DC 20205. (202)606-5000 (cns.gov).

INDEX

About the Author

Bruce Juell

Mr. Juell has been a U.S. Navy jet pilot, management consultant, turn-around specialist, investment banker, corporate CEO, venture capitalist, father, grandfather, a very poor golfer and an active volunteer.

After receiving his Bachelor of Engineering and MBA degrees from the University of Southern California, he joined the Los Angeles office of McKinsey & Company, where he worked in the areas of strategic and organizational planning. He founded Builders Resources Corporation and, as a key part of the Penn Central Railroad turnaround team, he served as CEO of Great Southwest Corporation and its wholly-owned subsidiary, Six Flags, Inc.

He was head of the Corporate Finance Department at Bateman Eichler, Hill Richards and held various consulting and management roles as CEO and/or president of Olson Farms, Inc., First City Properties, Inc., Kratos Corporation, IDM Corporation and R.A. Rowan & Co. Other consulting experience included projects with the Fidelity Group in Boston and Executive Life Insurance Company.

He has served on the Boards of Directors of Del Webb Corporation, IDM Corporation, Great Southwest Corporation, First City Properties, Arvida Corporation, AMCAP Mutual Fund, Olson Farms, Inc., Kratos Corporation, Bateman Eichler, Hill Richards and R.A. Rowan & Co.

He has been active in a number of business and community groups, including the Young Presidents' Organization, the Chief Executives' Organization, the Urban Land Institute, the UCLA School of Architecture Advisory Council, the California Club, the USC Entrepreneurial Program Advisory Board, the City of Hope Board of Governors, the House Ear Institute Foundation Board, Little Company of Mary Foundation, the Museum of Flying Board of Directors, Los Angeles Biomedical Research Institute and the Advancement Board of the Emeriti Center at the University of Southern California.

He and his wife Jean live in Palos Verdes Estates, California.

Order Form

Fax orders: 310-541-3595. Send a copy of this form
Telephone orders: 310-408-6427
email orders: orders@retirement-activities.com
Mail orders: 3rd Age Press
                 609 Deep Valley Road, Suite 200
                 Rolling Hills Estates, CA 90274

Please send the following:

_____

_____

_____

Name   _____

Address _____

City   _____ State____ Zip _____

Telephone _____ email _____

Shipping by air
   U.S.: $4.00 for first item, $2.00 for each additional item
   International: $9.00 for first item, $5.00 for each additional item

Payment: ❏ check   ❏ credit card

Card Type _____ Number _____

   Name   _____ exp: _____

Signature _____